Adoor Gopalakrishnan

ADOOR GOPALAKRISHNAN

A LIFE IN CINEMA

Gautaman Bhaskaran

Foreword by
Adoor Gopalakrishnan

PENGUIN
VIKING

VIKING
Published by the Penguin Group
Penguin Books India Pvt. Ltd, 11 Community Centre, Panchsheel Park,
New Delhi 110 017, India
Penguin Group (USA) Inc., 375 Hudson Street, New York, New York 10014, USA
Penguin Group (Canada), 90 Eglinton Avenue East, Suite 700, Toronto,
Ontario, M4P 2Y3, Canada (a division of Pearson Penguin Canada Inc.)
Penguin Books Ltd, 80 Strand, London WC2R 0RL, England
Penguin Ireland, 25 St Stephen's Green, Dublin 2, Ireland
(a division of Penguin Books Ltd)
Penguin Group (Australia), 250 Camberwell Road, Camberwell,
Victoria 3124, Australia (a division of Pearson Australia Group Pty Ltd)
Penguin Group (NZ), 67 Apollo Drive, Rosedale, North Shore 0632,
New Zealand (a division of Pearson New Zealand Ltd)
Penguin Group (South Africa) (Pty) Ltd, 24 Sturdee Avenue, Rosebank,
Johannesburg 2196, South Africa

Penguin Books Ltd, Registered Offices: 80 Strand, London WC2R 0RL, England

First published in Viking by Penguin Books India 2010

Copyright © Gautaman Bhaskaran 2010
Foreword copyright © Adoor Gopalakrishnan 2010

Photographs courtesy of Adoor Gopalakrishnan and Gautaman Bhaskaran

ISBN 9780670081714

Typeset in Sabon Roman by SÜRYA, New Delhi
Printed at Gopsons Papers Ltd, Noida

To my mother

Contents

Foreword

A journalist is turning a biographer with this book. Not an easy proposition, though many may think otherwise. In fact, there is nothing in common with the professional demands of a journalist's pursuit here.

A newspaper 'story' is for quick and casual consumption. One's skills are directed towards filling the allotted columns as a deadline hangs like a threat and a test. With the day's newspaper on the stands, yesterday's hot story is already old and cold.

A book, on the other hand, can make claims to a permanence of sorts. Once bought (even borrowed), it enjoys a special space on the reading table, as well as your travel bag, and before long it gets elevated to the shelf rubbing covers with others in seemingly safe preservation.

A book, no wonder, saddles the author with multiple responsibilities. Most importantly, its significance should survive the publication of another book on the same subject. In fact, a good biography should stand the scrutiny of authenticity, be rich in its material, and original in its observations, providing a firm ground for further study and analysis.

Even a detailed and painstakingly written book on an author or artist can fall short of being complete in every respect as there is always scope for further probe and understanding.

Articulation is not always the gift an artist has, as he or she reveals mostly through his or her art. While being a good listener, I must admit, I am a reluctant talker. In writing this book, Mr Gautaman Bhaskaran has mostly depended on my talk. Never before have I talked so much in my life, definitely not about myself.

The second part of this book deals with my films individually. It gives vital information about the making of each film along with some important details.

Gautaman has done well in not trying to be analytical about the films. It needs to be conceded that most of my films do not lend themselves to simple paraphrasing. Their ambition extends beyond mere storytelling. A wrong stress on any aspect of its thematic concerns can lead the reader astray. For instance, to approach *Nizhalkkuthu* (Shadow Kill) as a film against capital punishment would be too simplistic.

This book, I believe, will throw some light on my life and work. And I am happy it does as much.

8 April 2010   **Adoor Gopalakrishnan**
Thiruvananthapuram

Preface

It was many years ago that I met Gopalakrishnan from Adoor. It was so long ago that I do not remember when. I do not even recollect my first meeting with this auteur–director. But it was not at Adoor, where he was born. No, certainly not.

There is one meeting I remember distinctly. On a cold winter morning at New Delhi's Siri Fort, I ran into him. Literally. I was rushing in to catch the first movie of the day during the International Film Festival of India, which that year had returned to the capital, an alternate year stop for this gypsy event that has since then found a permanent home in Panaji.

Gopalakrishnan was beaming, his face lit up by the shy warmth of the early morning sun. As we exchanged greetings, he looked at me and asked, 'Gautaman, how come you look younger every time I see you?' I did not even pause to think before the words flew out of me. 'The magic of cinema, sir,' I said. And we laughed, both of us enslaved by the same overwhelming passion.

Years later, Gopalakrishnan has still not lost his sense of humour or the tinkle in his laughter. He can laugh like a child, oblivious of the world. In a Chennai hotel months ago, during one of my innumerable sessions with him for this biography, a telephone call from his wife interrupted our conversation. A few minutes later, I saw him burst out laughing, and he continued laughing for what seemed like a long time. He told me later that a prank by his grandson, Tashi—who is living with his police-officer parents in Maharashtra—had virtually tickled him out of shape. The two-year-old boy had jumped off a table and bruised his knee, and when the doctor came to take a look at him, Tashi was all set to re-enact his feat! The lad was already into his first movie takes!

Gopalakrishnan's cinema is often filled with humour that is neither lurid nor loud. Narayanan in *Naalu Pennungal* (Four Women) is such a glutton that we cannot help laughing at his undivided attention to his food-filled banana leaf, and the wit is so subtle and British I would think. Above all, it can be an effective way of building a character. At France's Deauville, where this film was screened in March 2008, I saw an essentially French audience enjoy Narayanan's tryst with food even as they empathized with Kumari's and Kamakshi's plight in the same work.

His work draws universal appreciation. Whether it is his native Kerala, where he was born and where he grew up to make his first movies, or Europe or America, his work is loved. For it talks about you and me. Often his hero is an ordinary man, like Sankarankutty in *Kodiyettam* (The Ascent), balding and shabbily attired. A simpleton, whom one writer called 'Peter Pan'. Or, it can be Ajayan in *Anantaram* (Monologue), defeated by an illness, or it may even be Kaliyappan in *Nizhalkkuthu* (Shadow Kill), reluctant to execute and guilt-ridden. These are men who do not exactly fit into the general celluloid concept of a hero, and they can be there out on the streets, one among the millions, faceless and maybe fractured, not flawed. When they are transported to the screen, they get a name, a face, a personality, and they help spin a yarn.

But the yarn can be a mere excuse to probe the complexities of the larger community. *Kathapurushan* (The Man of the

Story) documents the history of the period it is set in, and we see social and political developments through the eyes of the film's protagonist. *Mathilukal* (The Walls) takes us into a jail during the British Raj, and a canvas of relationships between the prisoners and the police and among the inmates themselves is presented in its stark reality. No grease paint and artifice here.

One of the most critically acclaimed directors after Satyajit Ray, Gopalakrishan's cinema is rooted in the Kerala milieu and often mirrors the community's concerns. He goes into its history—though usually not beyond the 1940s, the period he understands best for that is the one he has lived through—to elaborate social situations and orders. To explain these, he examines the individual minutely: his pains and pleasures are laid bare. Gopalakrishnan saw the decline of feudalism, and he showed us how clinging to its vestiges could ruin men like Unni in *Elippathayam* (The Rat-Trap) and Bhaskara Patelar in *Vidheyan* (The Servile).

Many of his male characters are weak, typical of this transitional period, when men were unsure of themselves, and just did not know what lay ahead. Unni is a good example of this. So is Sankarankutty in *Kodiyettam* (The Ascent). However, he moves from being a listless and lazy wastrel to a responsible and aware husband and father. Again, *Mukhamukham*'s (Face to Face) Sreedharan turns from a revered hero to a despicable drunkard.

Gopalakrishnan's cinema is subtle, yet forceful. Adoor has told me several times that he is a reluctant speaker, and this unwillingness to speak much is apparent in his work. A lot is left unsaid. We do now know why the couple in *Swayamvaram* (One's Own Choice) had to elope. Do they not have friends who could have helped them with money in their troubled days? Whom does Sridevi in *Elippathayam* run away with? We can only guess.

The Marxists were very uncomfortable with Gopalakrishnan's

silence when he was shooting *Mukhamukham*. They read meanings into it. However, this turned out to be his most widely commented work, and the director talked and gave detailed explanations, telling his critics that it was not a political movie. Rather, it was a story of a human being. But not everybody was convinced, and the noted film critic, the late Iqbal Masud, wrote: 'He (Sreedharan) is an individual in the process of disintegrating, and this is conveyed so powerfully that one sees in his ruined face and body, the ruins of a once-bright Communism.'

In *Vidheyan*, Saroja could have so easily raved and ranted at her husband's philandering and monstrous ways. But she does nothing of the sort. Instead, she is seen as her husband Patelar's quiet conscience. The effect of this is delicate yet telling, and even a brute like Patelar is agonized over the possibility of his wife having seen him as he kills her.

Interestingly, such subtlety comes from a man who spent all his youth dreaming of the stage—writing plays, performing in them and reading about them for a whole year when he was supposed to be learning cinema!

Added to this, Gopalakrishan's family was a patron of Kathakali. The family supported and maintained troupes. Yet, his cinema turned out to be a sheer visual experience, shorn of dramatic exaggeration that we see in many Indian films. Understated and multi-layered, his movies may appear simple at first. Often intricately woven, his stories cover a wide gamut of plots from unconventional relationships to schizophrenia to guilt to crime and sexual mores.

And when accolades came to him, including France's Commander of the Order of Arts and Letters in 2004, the Dada Saheb Phalke Award in 2005 and the Padma Vibhushan in 2006, they only seconded what every common man and woman, who has seen Gopalakrishnan's cinema, has long known. The man's work is fascinating.

It has been my endeavour to illuminate all this in this book.

I have tried to make it descriptive and informative work. As the first full-length biography of Adoor Gopalakrishnan in English, the book's reach would hopefully extend beyond the Kerala borders and whet the appetite for his cinema.

Acknowledgements

A door Gopalakrishnan, for the warmth and patience with which he told me his life story—extraordinary for a person who prefers to let his art speak for him. He not only spent hours patiently answering my queries, but pored over the manuscript making significant suggestions and corrections in order to ensure that the work turned out factually correct.

Ganesan Balachander, representative of the Ford Foundation in New Delhi, who helped me secure a travel grant from his organization that facilitated my research for this book. I had to journey several times to Thiruvananthapuram, Pune and other Indian cities to watch Adoor's cinema and gather material on him.

Udayan Mitra, of Penguin Books India, who instantly understood the value of a tome on Gopalakrishnan, and in a matter of minutes on my first meeting with him in New Delhi agreed to publish a book whose first word had not been written.

N. Ravi, Editor of *The Hindu*, Chennai, whose immensely warm professional encouragement enabled me to travel across continents and cover film festivals for many, many years. Through this exposure, I learnt to appreciate cinema, different kinds of it, and fully understood the beauty of the 'other cinema', of which auteur-directors like Adoor are an integral part. In fact, there was one defining moment when Ravi stepped in and made it possible for me to write this book.

Sasidharan, Director, Pune's National Film Archive of India, who responded to this project by screening Adoor's movies and providing access to the library.

Sreekanth M. Girinath, who spent hours transcribing my innumerable interviews.

E.P. Unny, cartoonist and dear friend, who years ago introduced me to Malayalam cinema and to some of its great helmers, such as G. Aravindan and Adoor, and to his very useful guidance.

Rohit, my son, who was the first to read my manuscript. As one whose core interest is not exactly cinema, his incisive observations proved invaluable to me. I have incorporated many of his suggestions, and hope that I would be able to convert some like him into fans of meaningful movies.

Manju, my wife, who patiently stood by me during those difficult days of my research and writing.

1

Feet on the Earth

The Indian monsoon can be terrifying. Menacing grey clouds, blinding flashes of lightning and deafening thunder transform the landscape into wild expanses of water that wash away men and material, often in a trail of destruction and despair. It was on one such afternoon—when the skies had opened up in all their fury—that a woman in a remote south Indian village went into labour. The pain grew acute as the rain lashed mercilessly, and her spasms came in ever increasing frequency. The birth seemed difficult, awfully difficult, and Gouri Kunjamma knew that of all her deliveries this was going to be the most arduous. Day turned into night, and there was no sign of the child. The woman grew desperate, longing to hear the cry of her baby, a cry that would free her from intense agony but enslave her to love and joy.

Finally, as the night was beginning to break into dawn, the child arrived, feet first, in what is called a breech delivery, quite oblivious of the storm he had created in that house.

Outside, there were two kinds of storms raging. One was caused by the monsoon, and the other rose against subjugation

1

and slavery. For the British who had colonized India for decades, the gathering freedom movement seemed more frightening than tempests. Mahatma Gandhi's resolve to free the nation from foreign yoke culminated in the Quit India movement, and threatened to crush British bandooks and babudom. Gandhi's satyagraha was starting to evoke a never-seen-before patriotism. No corner could remain untouched by it, including Kerala's Pallickal, renowned for its paddy farmers, Nair community and good-hearted people. It is there and among such genial souls that Adoor Gopalakrishnan was born to Gouri Kunjamma on the third day of July 1941.

Pallickal lay on the periphery of Adoor, the headquarters of Kunnathoor taluk in Quilon district of the erstwhile State of Travancore. Today it is part of Kerala. Pallickal drew its energy from Adoor, which even in the mid-1900s had government offices, a law court, a hospital and a high school. In fact, the region around Adoor, made up of a cluster of villages, was commonly called Adoor, and artists and writers from there used the name as a prefix. And they were proud of it.

Pallickal's dark skies that day in July seemed like a harbinger of the coming calamity. Gandhi's non-violent path was often smeared with hatred and blood. India's Partition, in particular, caused one of the greatest human tragedies the world has ever known. Even Gandhi, whose very presence had mesmeric power, could do little to stop the murder and mayhem.

Gopalakrishnan must have been moved profoundly by these, even affected, and it is not surprising that he developed very early in life a strong attraction for Gandhian ideology and a fascination for khadi. And along with these his passion for theatre grew, but at some point, the screen eclipsed the stage, theatrics mellowing into a subtle and sober cinematic idiom.

His birth that had all the ingredients of drama led to a life which was as dramatic, sometimes exhilaratingly so, sometimes poignantly so. Breech deliveries are the most difficult of childbirths—when the feet or the buttocks of a baby arrive first. Adoor says jocularly 'that is why I have my feet on the earth'. And quite firmly too, I would think.

Gopalakrishnan pictures this scene in his *Kathapurushan* (The Man of the Story, 1995), where the protagonist Kunjunni is born feet first. The family astrologer examines the child's horoscope and predicts grim times for him—pain and a childhood without paternal care. The film draws considerably from the director's own life—as we will see—and he even uses the same house in Pallickal where he was born, though not the same room.

He says many large households had a labour room where children cried their first breath. It used to be one of the best ventilated, but now, with babies being born in hospitals and nursing homes, the space has been put to other uses. Sometimes it is used as a kitchen, as in the Pallickal house.

Gopalakrishnan was the sixth child in a large family of three girls and four boys, though one of them had died as a child long before Adoor was born. Gopalakrishnan grew to be the most gifted of the children—a celebrated cinema auteur, a grand Indian.

His beginnings probably held a clue or two to the greatness that lay in him. His single-minded pursuit of goals very early in life certainly said something. He was fearless as he was adventurous, often deeply focussing, much like the way he has been wielding the megaphone, on attainment and accomplishment.

There is a story of the ten-year-old Gopalakrishnan diving into the well of his house at Adoor, where his family moved for the convenience of education. He did not drown, but rose above the water and held on with his arms and legs to the sides of the well till help arrived in the form of burly men.

Once he was out of the well, he says, he ran far away from home, his childish fears of being rebuked overtaking him at that point. He returned much later in the day when the family had forgotten all about the traumatic incident, and one supposes that no one even scolded him, let alone spank him.

Often, while his mother would give him an oil massage in the courtyard, he would dart after a speeding squirrel, the oil aiding in his quick getaway, and would end up falling flat and hurting himself. One sees a similar scene in *Kathapurushan.* The young Kunjunni falls on muddy ground, his face lacerated and oozing with blood. The cook's little daughter, Meenakshi, giggles at this, but later consoles and comforts him.

On other occasions, little Gopalakrishnan would climb a mango tree and go for the fruit perched at the end of a branch. His desire for the mango would be so intense, and his concentration to get it so singular, that he would forget that the poor branch could not carry his weight. It would snap, and he would fall to the ground—mango, leaves, branch and all— with a loud thud.

His mother working in the kitchen grew so accustomed to her son's falls that she would know the moment she heard a thump what had happened. She would rush out, armed with a bowl of herbal oil, and lovingly apply it on his body to ease the pain.

The memory of his mother soothing him with a balm of love endures to this day in Adoor's mind. But I do not remember any film of his that captures this. Perhaps it is too precious, too close to his heart, to share it with his audiences.

It is clear when he talks to me that his mother was dearest to him. She was warm and kind, and would be the last to have her food, waiting for that unexpected and tired visitor. She could never let anyone go away hungry. 'She was an innocent soul,' Adoor reminisces, 'but spirited and courageous nevertheless, and lived by her convictions.'

Gopalakrishnan's father, Madhavan Unnithan, was a forest ranger who frequently moved from one patch of green to another, and Gouri Kunjamma would travel with him, something women of Kerala's Nair gentry, to which she belonged, did not do in those days. They seldom left home. In fact, the husband would visit his wife at her house (her mother's house), and live with her. The matrilineal line of succession and way of life were the established norm then, at least among some communities, the Nairs certainly, the clan that Gopalakrishnan comes from.

Gouri Kunjamma, however, chose to ignore some aspects of matrilocality while adhering to some others. She was fiercely independent in a sense, perhaps a cause of her unhappy marriage.

In her later years, she was separated from her husband, and raised her children all by herself. Although the family had large landed properties and was quite well-to-do, it faced enormous hardship because there was no man around. 'My mother had real problems, because those who worked for her cheated her,' Adoor tells me.

He was twenty-one when she died of cancer in 1962. Her death followed long spells of hospitalization at Thiruvananthapuram, the second occasion in her life she was forced to live away from home.

Earlier at her Pallickal house, she had a bad fall when a steep wooden staircase collapsed. She fractured her shoulder and had to be taken by road to Thiruvananthapuram for medical treatment that lasted two-and-a-half years. Gopalakrishnan says he still remembers the car journey from Pallickal. His mother's eldest brother, Mouttathu Gopalan Unnithan, owned one of those fancy Ford cars whose canvas top could be folded, but the vehicle broke down on the way. He had to get a lorry to tow the car all the way to his house at Adoor, where a visibly distraught Gouri Kunjamma was given some sort of first aid and the car mended. Finally, she reached the General Hospital in Thiruvananthapuram, a long journey in those days, particularly torturous in her condition. But she never complained, stoically bearing the excruciating pain.

By then her marriage had broken, though the couple did not formally divorce. Gopalakrishnan, then barely into his ninth year, despite living amongst a host of relatives that included his cousins, uncles and aunts, felt like an orphan, a fact that conveys his closeness to his mother. And he suffered. Even the servants differentiated between him and the other children, because his parents were not around.

Madhavan Unnithan would visit his wife and children once in a way, but it is apparent that he was not much of an influence on Gopalakrishnan. A university graduate in those days—when graduates were comparatively rare and graduation itself was considered a remarkable achievement—Madhavan Unnithan joined the Travancore Forest Department as a ranger and strangely retired as a ranger. Normally, a graduate ranger would be expected to rise in rank and perhaps retire as a conservator of forests. It is presumed that he never got along with his seniors, and this impeded his professional progress.

After retirement, he became a teacher, a very popular one at that, and taught English in a college at Changanassery, close to Kottayam. Later, he gave private tuitions assuring students of academic success. And he delivered, teaching till his last days. He was eighty-six when he died in 1984, a man loved and idolized by his students, though not quite by his family.

Madhavan was an Unnithan, a special title bestowed on some Nairs of Travancore, a princely State in British India. In fact, only Nairs could join the Travancore army, and only Unnithans could captain them. The Unnithans were a kind of nobility who enjoyed royal patronage.

Naturally, the Unnithans wielded considerable clout in society, and young Gopalakrishnan grew up fancying himself as privileged. Maybe, he took an astrologer's prediction seriously: He would grow up to be the Captain of the Travancore State cavalry. Indeed, he did become one, though of cinema—a far more challenging job.

As a child too, he had some memorable times. He particularly remembers his days at Veeyapuram in Kerala's Kuttanad in Alappuzha district where Madhavan Unnithan was posted. His office and living quarters were adjacent, but Gopalakrishnan's most unforgettable image is that of a nearby timber warehouse that stood by the Pampa, which merged with two other rivers, the Achankovil and the Manimala, to widen and flow into the Vembanad Lake.

He went to Veeyapuram as recently as 2007 when he was shooting *Naalu Pennungal* (Four Women) at Ambalappuzha, also in Kerala's Alappuzha district, renowned for its backwater and houseboat tourism. He was surprised to see his father's quarters and office still there, though they were dilapidated and unused. The quarters' thatched roof remains. It had not been tiled like the office. People preferred thatch to tile because it kept the indoors cool in summer. Those were the days when even fans were uncommon, let alone air conditioners.

There are some more pictures of Veeyapuram that Gopalakrishnan still treasures. One of them is of a pot-bellied priest who would sail in a *kodumbu vallam*, a small boat that could hold a single person, and the young boy from the veranda of his father's quarters could see the priest, not the craft. Shaped like the sheath of a coconut inflorescence or *kodumbu*, the *vallam* or the boat would almost submerge in water under the weight of the sailor, and from a distance it would appear as if the man alone was gliding by.

It was a ritual for the priest to sail by every day on his way to the Iyappan temple and it was a joy for Gopalakrishnan to watch him paddle past.

The boy accompanied his parents to even places now in Tamil Nadu, but which were then part of Travancore. At one such halt of his father's, Shenkottai, the Tamils working for the family would affectionately call Gopalakrishnan 'Gopali'. He says even now some relatives address him by that name.

Another image that still plays and replays in his mind is that of the weed-covered pond by his Pallickal house. He would go

there every morning for his bath and then to the adjacent
temple for prayers. His mother would keep watch, lest the lad
played pranks.

Much later in his life, when he wrote *Kathapurushan*, he
thought of the pond. One of the scenes was planned on the
steps leading to it—a meeting between Kunjunni and his love,
Meenakshi.

A few days before the shoot, Gopalakrishnan went to take
a look at the pond. To his amazement, he felt that it had
shrunk with time. He had not seen the pond in a few decades.
Obviously, his memory was playing tricks. The real was
eclipsed by the imagined. The pond did not become smaller,
but it had, over the years, grown larger in his inner eye.

2

Panning Places

Often, a building ceases to be mere brick and mortar. Or, wood and clay as they were earlier. As the walls begin to feel the warmth of human breath, and the floors the gentle weight of our footsteps, the structure pulsates. It springs to life, and an overwhelming bond grows between the pile of stones and mortals like us. The edifice stands, silently watching men and women as they live out their lives. Etched on each brick, each beam and on each crevice are memories of an era gone by. Gopalakrishnan's early homes at Pallickal and Adoor have captivating stories.

Medayil, the Pallickal house where he was born, belonged to his maternal grandfather. It was a palatial two-storey building that to the little boy seemed to rise majestically out of lush paddy fields and coconut groves.

He used to wonder why his family built a home that far from a town. Later, he realized that the family's business centred on its farmlands, and constant supervision was necessary, particularly during the sowing and harvesting of grain.

There were no motorcars when the house was built over a

hundred years ago, and bullock carts were the only means of surface transport. Kerala's innumerable rivers, canals and lakes fed by copious rain helped waterways to thrive as an alternative form of conveyance.

The family used a bullock cart to move around. Bullocks were specially bred and reared for this task. The cart had springs—call them suspension in today's parlance—and it was termed *villu vandi* (spring cart).

One such cart can be seen in the backyard of Gopalakrishnan's Thiruvananthapuram house, Darsanam. The cart was used in his 2002 film *Nizhalkkuthu* (Shadow Kill), the one that transported the hangman and his son to the jail where a convict awaited capital punishment. The cart reminds visitors to the director's home of an extremely disturbing movie that studies an executioner's guilt and remorse. I would think for the first time in Indian cinema, maybe even in world cinema, that human guilt has been depicted with such intensity.

A two-storey structure such as Medayil was uncommon in those days. Gopalakrishnan's grandparents built it to celebrate the birth of their youngest son at the start of the 1900s. It had light blue floors that gleamed like mirror. Ingredients such as egg white, coconut shells and indigo powder were used to get a finish of this kind. Some of the seventeenth, eighteenth and nineteenth century Kerala buildings, including the Padmanabhapuram Palace (constructed around 1600), about 65 km from Thiruvananthapuram, had similar floors. Medayil even had a bathroom on the first floor, a rarity then.

The edifice was a novelty, and people from far away came to have a glimpse of it. I can picture a scene where passers-by would have stopped to stare—and been awestruck. I remember a somewhat similar curiosity that Chennai's (Madras then) fourteen-storey Life Insurance Corporation building evoked once. Probably once the tallest in south India, it was a landmark that attracted visitors from neighbouring towns and villages.

At Medayil, it was not just the curious who came by. Dancers, musicians and even magicians paid a visit to it, stayed for some days as guests and performed after sunset. Renowned violinist T.N. Krishnan once told Adoor that he had visited Medayil with his father and guru or teacher, A. Narayana Iyer, who gave a recital. Iyer belonged to a family whose musical lineage could be traced back to five generations.

Chenganoor Raman Pillai (16 January 1886–11 November 1980), a Kathakali celebrity and Travancore Palace dancer, had also been to Medayil, staying there as part of a troupe Gopalakrishnan's family supported. In 1974, when he shot a documentary on Chenganoor (as he was customarily known), then eighty-eight, he embraced the helmer and expressed delight at having met three generations of his family—maternal grandfathers (Gopalakrishnan's grandmother had two husbands, both brothers, and polyandry was a socially accepted norm then), their children and the grandson himself.

After the grandfathers died, Medayil was abandoned, and the grandmother along with her family moved back to Mouttathu, her own *tharavadu* (Hindu Nair matrilineal joint family house) at Adoor, its good educational facilities being the primary reason for this shift. The house was a sprawling *naalukettu*, a traditional architecture with rooms built around a rectangular courtyard opening out to the sky. Well ventilated, the naalukettu interiors remained cool even at the height of summer. Some thirty men, women and children lived there. Despite its spaciousness, there was not enough room for everybody, and several people had to share a single room.

Gopalakrishnan's memories of this house are not exactly pleasant. This is where he felt like an orphan with his mother away in Thiruvananthapuram to get her broken shoulder treated. This is also where he saw the disintegration and decay of the matrilineal system and the tharavadu. 'I was born at a time when matrilocality was disappearing. In fact, I saw the last days of it,' Adoor tells me sitting in his study whose walls are lined with hundreds of books on hundreds of subjects. Dictionaries, anthologies and biographies rub shoulders with huge posters of *Naalu Pennungal* (premiered in the prestigious Masters Section of the 2007 Toronto International Film Festival), attractively designed and brightly coloured to tickle public curiosity. Tomes on cinema and Kerala's culture call attention as well from another corner of the room. Hitchcock and Fellini ooze film. Kathakali catches my eye with the painted face hypnotizing me.

My mind, abstracted by the multitude of titles, is gently nudged back to the subject of matrilineal structure that traced its lineage through women. Even a part of the family property went to daughters. A man married into a woman's family, and lived in her house. Their children were looked after by uncles, the mother's brothers. It was their duty, but over a period of time, uncles, who were also married and had their own children, began to neglect their nephews and nieces. This happened despite the uncle–nephew tie being sanctified by marriage: a nephew could marry his uncle's daughter. In other words, a cousin could wed cousin.

Such a consanguineous marriage helped the family property to remain within the family. This I would suppose was the real reason. In the next-door state of Tamil Nadu, a man could marry his sister's daughter, despite the difference in age. Here also property was a consideration. The dowry—which the bride's family gave, and still gives, to the groom—remained within the clan.

In Kerala's matrilineal setup, particularly in the Nair community, there was no dowry. But it came later when joint families started to split. The Hindu Tamil Brahmin settlers as well as the local Christians apparently had a demonstration effect on the Nairs, who were turning patriarchal and nuclear. Some scholars have traced dowry in Kerala to this phase.

When Gopalakrishnan's parents left the Mouttathu tharavadu and settled down at Kaniyerathu, a house his father built on the land his mother owned, also at Adoor, the break-up of the joint family seemed imminent. Even a nuclear family like Madhavan Unnithan–Gouri Kunjamma's appeared to be under stress.

There were occasions when Gouri Kunjamma would go back to Medayil after a quarrel with her husband. The house was empty, its occupants, as we know, having moved away to Adoor. Except for a manager, there was no man there, but Gouri Kunjamma's fiery spirit did not allow much of a compromise with her husband. She would rather be lonely in a sense and stay in a rather desolate place than live with him. Initially, these partings were not for long, but I suppose a time came when the marriage hit beyond-the-repair mark.

After the informal separation of the couple, Gouri Kunjamma continued to live at Kaniyerathu, the house her husband built. 'You really cannot call this my father's house,' Adoor explains. 'The fact is that the land belonged to her. At that point in time, building a house was not a big deal like it is today. Even the laterite and wood used in the building came from the land. And labourers were paid not in cash, but in kind, usually paddy, which again came from my mother's fields. My father merely supervised the construction.' What is more, it was Gouri Kunjamma who completed the house over the years, and brought it to the shape that we see it in today.

Gopalakrishnan's journey from Kaniyarethu was a long one that eventually ended at Darsanam, his home now, and the story of how this house was conceived and constructed is enthralling.

'One day, a newspaper advertisement said an old Kerala wooden house in Thiruvananthapuram was being pulled down to make way for a cinema,' Adoor says. The house was about 200 years old, and the invaluable wood and other parts of the building were to be auctioned. The house once belonged to a senior Travancore Palace official, but had been sold and resold several times before it was bought by a hotelier. He must have had little use for a structure like this and decided that the land could be utilized more lucratively by opening a film theatre there.

Gopalakrishnan was always passionate about tradition and all things traditional. He grew up in conventional surroundings, and his disposition had been conditioned by them. So out of curiosity he went to the auction. Which was strange, because the bidders were merchants, men of hardcore figures with little feeling for history or heritage. They wanted to buy the wood and sell it as fuel, firewood to be precise. Gopalakrishnan must have felt awful at the thought of such prized wood going up in smoke, and along with it pages from the past.

The auction was not going well for the hotel owner, and the price offered was abysmally low. Quite naturally. The traders perhaps looked at the wood as mere fuel to light the home fire. They were not going to put a higher tag on it because it was antique. A point came when the sale was about to be called off. By then Gopalakrishnan must have been angry at such merciless merchandising. He stepped in, offered Rs 5000 more than the best bid and clinched the deal. As the hammer came down, its knock appeared to signal the birth of a house that he could call his very own. His real home.

He now had great material to build a house but not an inch of land. Indeed a strange predicament. He got the wood shifted to the compound of the Chitralekha Film Cooperative, which he and his college mate, Kulathoor Bhaskaran Nair, established in 1965 at Aakulam on Thiruvananthapuam's outskirts. The wood lay there for a whole year bruised by the sun and battered by rain before Gopalakrishnan could find the money and zero in on a plot, happily adjoining the Cooperative. Had not the wood begun to rot, he might have postponed buying the land and building Darsanam.

The process was laborious, because the wood had been painted several times over and was done to death with nails, and finding master craftsmen who knew the intricacies of erecting a traditional Kerala wooden house—which Gopalakrishnan planned—was difficult. It took eight months of struggle, supervision and several changes of craftsmen before Darsanam emerged, wood with wood, plank with plank, all blended into a harmonious whole. The year was 1977, and he has been living there for more than thirty years with his wife, Sunanda, and daughter, Aswati—now married and with her husband.

Today, Darsanam looks like a museum with pretty paintings, bright brassware and wonderful wood carvings. A mini rectangular courtyard in the hall opens out to the sky. Sometimes, the rain falls through it and at other times, the rays of the sun creep in. But at all times, a gentle breeze blows in.

The director once thought that there was ample room for his curio collections that multiplied after each movie or travel of his. But with artefact acquisitions quickly surpassing space, he is planning to build one more room to preserve his precious possessions.

Till then Darsanam may appear a little cluttered, yet artistic and aesthetic, with incandescent lamps—not tubelights, because they are harsh on the eye, claims Adoor—radiating an ethereal glow to let 'night feel like night'. And long into this night or any other, Gopalakrishnan dreams.

3

Picturing People

Gopalakrishnan made films about real people and real situations. There was nothing artificial or superficial about them. Not even pretentious. The characters were entirely believable. Madhu, the hero in Gopalakrishnan's first feature, *Swayamvaram* (One's Own Choice, 1972), once told me that while 'others made cinema, Adoor made life'. He recreated on the big screen men and women we meet every day, their joys and sorrows we are familiar with, their fortunes and misfortunes we can identify with, and their friendships and fights that are so common in our own existences.

All this he saw in and around his own life, in the community he lived. He had the great opportunity to meet and be with people whose interests were amazingly varied. And they came early into his life.

His aunt and Gouri Kunjamma's eldest sister, Kutty Kunjamma, wrote plays, her characters emerging out of her vivid imagination, enriched by Hindu mythology. Aware that Gopalakrishnan loved theatre, she would ask him, then twelve or thirteen, to read what she wrote and give his opinion. The boy dared not displease her. So he always gave her an excellent review, and she was happy, letting him use her library of great collections that included even works by Bengal's Bankimchandra Chattopadhyay and Saratchandra Chattopadhyay.

Another attraction at his aunt's place was the radio, which he saw for the first time. It ran on car battery, because there was no electricity at Nellimukal, midway between Pallickal and Adoor, where Kutty Kunjamma lived. Sunday mornings were special for him, because he could listen to *Bala Lokam* (The Young World) on the radio and take off on his flight of fancy. Though she was a stern matriarch in every sense of the term, quite the opposite of her younger sister, there was a lot of affection between the boy and his sixty-year-old aunt, the yawning gap bridged by the world of letters that both savoured.

Gopalakrishnan's family was as well read as it was cultured. One of his uncles, Gouri Kunjamma's eldest brother, Mouttathu Gopalan Unnithan, was a great patron of the arts, especially Kathakali. Some landed or wealthy families like Gopalakrishnan's supported large Kathakali troupes, often as a matter of interest and, at other times, as a sign of sophistication and aristocracy.

Kathakali is not just dance as is often believed. It is basically theatre. In fact, it is dance-theatre. And interestingly, it is pretty close to cinema in its eclectic content. It has music, which is descriptive as well as dialogue. It has mime that goes with its stylized form of *abhinaya* or acting. There are elements of painting and sculpture too in the rich and saturated colours of costumes and make-up. There is no mask used, but the actor's face is intricately painted to allow mobility facilitating the expression of various *bhava*s or feelings. At its traditional best, Kathakali has a single major source of light. Actors perform before a tall *attavilakku* or theatre lamp in unison with rhythmic drumming. The amber light from the flickering flames lends aura and mystery to the mythological characters. Words as well as ideas are acted out in *mudra*s or hand gestures in a dramatic way, always to the accompaniment of instrumental music. Adoor says had the Russian master, Sergei Eisenstein, witnessed a performance of Kathakali, he would not have turned to Kabuki for his inspiration to propound the theory of montage.

Gopalakrishnan's family was also committed to other art forms. His mother and sisters were initiated into music, and Gouri Kunjamma could even play the violin. It is another story that she lost touch with all this after her marriage, which brought about its own compulsions, and increasingly so when Madhavan Unnithan began to live away from her and his children.

Gopalan Unnithan, also Gopalakrishnan's guardian, was highly enterprising. He opened the first cinema theatre at Adoor—later he built a few more in neighbouring Enath and Parakkode—working with an electricity generator and a single projector, which meant that there were many intermissions, one every time the reel had to be changed. 'We used to call these intervals "end-reels", and the time was used by vendors to sell song-books [which included an outline of the movie's plot and the song lyrics], snacks and bottled fizzy drinks,' Adoor looks back on an experience that was delightfully different and maybe even immensely satisfying.

In fact, his uncle's cinema provided the first ever glimpse of moving pictures for the boy Gopalakrishnan. He remembers watching the first Malayalam talkie *Balan*. Although it was made in 1938, three years before he was born, he must have seen it later. In those days, very few Malayalam pictures were made, as infrequent as one in three or four years. Most theatres played Tamil fare, whose production in the 1930s, the 1940s and even later was impressive.

At his uncle's theatre, Gopalakrishnan did not have to buy a ticket, but the free entry came with one hassle that seemed 'too irksome'. There was this little problem of getting past the gatekeeper, whom Adoor jocularly refers to as *dwarapalaka* (the gatekeeper). He was never turned away, but it took a while for the keeper to recognize the lad when he came alone without the elders in his family.

Another of Gouri Kunjamma's elder brothers, Madhavan Unnithan, was an advocate. He went on to become a member of Kerala's first Legislative Assembly, and was a classmate of Gopalakrishnan's father (also Madhavan Unnithan), a friendship that could have led to his meeting and marrying Gouri Kunjamma.

Her younger brother, Mouttathu Raman Unnithan, was the most artistic in the family. A disciple of Raja Ravi Varma's son, Rama Varma, Raman Unnithan studied painting and sculpting. He painted lifelike backdrops for the plays he wrote, and drew biting political cartoons for a Malayalam newspaper.

Gopalakrishnan would be one of his first readers. Though there was a good thirty-year difference in age between the two, the older man would share with his nephew the plays he penned. Raman Unnithan appreciated the boy's interest in theatre. 'Even as a schoolboy I was writing and presenting plays,' Adoor says. 'In fact, I began writing when I was barely ten.'

Raman Unnithan was truly a man of myriad interests, a colourful personality whose wit and laughter were infectious. Passionate about photography, he would often freeze members of his family into sombre statuesque stillness. If he was not clicking, he was playing chess, commanding his army towards victory, and anybody, just anybody, who could fight him on the chequered field, was fed and favoured, even pampered and patronized. Away from scheming kings and queens, and the marches of foot soldiers, horses and elephants, he dreamt, sometimes of converting copper into gold. But he could never hit upon a way to do that, and a solution eluded him all his life. But he was a character who could have easily popped out of a Marquez story.

The fourth uncle, Mouttathu Raghavan Unnithan, unlike his brothers, whiled away his life. He did not even marry. He thought that taking up a job or working for somebody else was an insult to his lineage. 'He spent his entire life criticizing, especially his innovative elder brother,' I can trace a note of regret in Adoor.

When he made *Elippathayam* (The Rat-Trap) in 1981, it was generally believed that he had modelled Unni (essayed by Karamana Janardhanan Nair)—the wimpish landlord confined to his home and shamelessly dependent on his sister, Rajamma— on his fourth uncle. Raghavan Unnithan may have been the 'starting point or a subconscious inspiration for Unni, but nothing beyond that', Adoor explains. He, however, admits, 'After all, your work is about yourself, your experiences, your problems, your dilemmas. What you want to tell others depends on your own likes and dislikes, your prejudices and tolerances. Often, you may not be conscious of them, but then that is the truth,' Adoor reflects on his cinema.

Actually, Karamana , a close friend of Gopalakrishnan, was unlike Unni, who was self-centred to the point of being obsessed with himself. Karamana, on the other hand, never took care of himself. I remember Adoor telling me that the actor generally lacked discipline, indulged in excesses and died early.

However, he could be extraordinarily regimented when he wanted to. Here is what Adoor wrote about him in a Malayalam book of articles collectively titled *Cinema Anubhavam* (Cinema as Experience): 'He [Karamana] has acted in many movies, but his role in *Elippathayam* is something that comes once in a lifetime for an artiste. He really worked hard to play Unni, starving himself to get that haggard look'. A frugal diet was prescribed for him by Adoor, and the actor stuck to it with uncharacteristic discipline. A week before the shooting began, he was found surviving on rice gruel, and he 'transformed himself into a perfect Unni with sunken eyes, gaunt cheeks and a lean frame to resemble the character as he appears towards the end.' (Gopalakrishnan shot the final scenes of *Elippathayam* first to picture a starved Karamana. As the work progressed from the end to the middle to the beginning, Karamana gradually went back to his normal diet and looks.)

For all the torture he subjected himself to, the fruits, when they came, were really sweet. Karamana became synonymous with *Elippathayam*, a high point in Gopalakrishnan's opus, and people remembered the actor's face at the very mention of this work. Unni was so unforgettable and so popular that his heart surgeon carried out a major procedure without delays or hassles when Karamana took critically ill.

When he was convalescing after the traumatic surgery, Gopalakrishnan and Sunanda went to see him. Since Karamana's house had remained locked during his hospitalization, rats had taken over the place much to the annoyance of his wife. But he was far from irritated, and saw humour in the situation, despite being weak and in pain. 'These rats are from *Elippathayam*. They have come to see me,' quipped Karamana, and everybody roared with laughter. Gopalakrishnan too, but he was at the same time overcome with emotion. 'Tears welled up in my eyes, and I tried to hide them from others,' Adoor talks about Karamana, whom he describes as an outstanding artist (*Swayamvaram*, *Mukhamukham*, and *Mathilukal*, apart from *Elippathayam*.) and, above all, a fine human being.

He was undoubtedly close to Gopalakrishnan, acting in his plays and later in his films, and even teaching him to ride a scooter, not on a movie set but on a real road! The lessons were by the seashore, adjoining Thiruvananthapuram airport. It took just two hours for the director to learn riding; he already knew how to cycle having mastered the art of balancing when he was in school, and that helped. He had a fairly good road sense and the rest was simple. Adoor says he was confident enough to let Karamana ride pillion at the end of the two-hour class in a reversal of roles. The director had arrived at the beach on the pillion, but left riding the two-wheeler.

The scooter bought by his elder brother, Ramachandran Unnithan, was of no use to him by the time it was delivered— eight years after it was booked. Those were times when one had to wait endlessly even for a telephone connection. So the brother gave the vehicle to Gopalakrishnan soon after he returned from the Pune Film Institute of India (now called Film and Television Institute of India). It became his 'official vehicle', and he used it for many years, even transporting heavy film reels on it and generally spreading the magic of movies.

Ramachandran Unnithan was a writer as well. He had a flair for short stories, but could not pursue his interest because he had to take charge of the household after the family patriarch Gopalan Unnithan died. A professor of botany at the Pandalam Nair Service Society College (popularly called NSS College, where Gopalakrishnan studied), Ramachandran Unnithan used to act in amateur plays, even English. Shakespeare was his favourite, and he often had major roles. 'In fact, as a boy I was basically imitating this brother of mine, some years older to me,' Adoor talks about one of his early and important inspirations. 'He was a voracious reader. In fact, most members of my family were avid readers, and there were times during the day when each one of us would retreat to a corner in the house with a book. Somebody walking in then would feel that it was not a house but a library.'

Gopalakrishnan as a schoolboy had, along with a group of friends and relatives, set up a library and an arts club in his village. The library movement in Kerala was unique in the country, contributing to the region's literacy and general awareness. Even a remote village had a library, which often published a literary magazine that was handwritten, not printed. These magazines apart from containing an intriguing collection of handwritings, provided budding writers, poets and illustrators with a platform. Gopalakrishnan wrote as well, sometimes poetry. 'Very recently, one of my nephews recited a poem written by me many, many years ago. It was a translation in

Malayalam of William Cowper's "The Nightingale and the Glow-Worm" [originally written in English in 1780 and published two years later],' Adoor says.

When he finished his course at the film institute in the early 1960s, it was his brother who supported him for those long years when Gopalakrishnan struggled to make cinema. Those days, it was difficult to make even documentaries. Nobody was willing to commission them. 'My brother was very patient. While the rest of the world kept asking me why I was not taking up a job, he never bothered me with that question. He understood me. He had complete faith in me,' Adoor is happy to have had such an understanding sibling.

For him, the most awe-inspiring of all his relatives was Gopalan Unnithan. He was an 'amazing person in many ways'. In all of central Travancore, he was one of the very few to buy a car, but his reckless driving often proved perilous to fellow riders. There were instances of his car, packed with friends and family, going out of control and plunging into a river. Fortunately, nobody ever died or was seriously hurt, and the car was invariably salvaged.

Despite these mishaps, his uncle never got tired of either changing his car or going for a spin that sometimes spun out of control. 'There were days when he would take us all—no less than eighteen men, women and children—in his car to the pictures. The cars were huge and expensive (one cost about Rs 35,000, and in the 1950s this was quite a sum), and ranged from Ford to Chevrolet . . . The cars even had footboards on which some of us would ride,' Adoor cruises down memory lane. He remembers watching movies such as *Pathala Bhairavi* (Old is Gold), *Haridas* and *Jhanak Jhanak Payal Bhaje* (The Ring of the Anklet). Truly cinematic these incidents, and probably little Gopalakrishnan's mind was storing all these images to be recalled and reframed later.

Cars apart, his family had another fancy—elephants. An elephant was a status symbol, and a rich and powerful family normally had a couple of these animals, but it would forever be seeking to acquire more, particularly those that were well bred or looked handsome. And the length a family would go to possess a prized elephant was incredible. There was one occasion when Gopalakrishnan's maternal grandfathers literally stole a tusker from one who had refused to sell it. The men had made up their minds that the animal, a majestic creature, must be theirs, and the great elephant robbery became the juiciest scandal of the region, finally pushing the brothers into the dock. However, the court declared them innocent. The judgement was undoubtedly a slap on justice that favoured the more influential of the two sides in the dispute, but so what, the brothers got the tusker and went back home trumpeting.

A *thullal katha* (a highly developed semi-classical art form, where stories are narrated through song and dance) called *Gajendra Vijayam* (Victory of the Elephant) was written and performed, much to the glee of the old men.

When they were not eyeing elephants, they amused themselves by performing magic or just watching a classical recital, and Gopalakrishnan remembers his mother talking about a strange feat of theirs. Some *kaakkan*s (wandering entertainers, who often played tricks) had produced hens (out of thin air) and let them loose on a large quantity of grain spread out to dry on the Medayil courtyard. When the magician-grandfather saw this, he quickly retaliated with a fox (which also appeared out of nowhere) that made a meal of the poor birds to the utter disbelief and dismay of the kaakkans.

Gopalakrishnan listened to stories like this with the typical curiosity of a boy finding his feet in the wide world where fact mixed and mingled with fiction, where both goodness and badness existed like Siamese twins, where might conflicted with right. Often, he was bewildered, and struggled to find the line between the two.

As we watch his films, we begin to understand the choices he made, the choices he fought for and stuck to. Very early on, he decided the kind of life he would lead, a life shorn of excesses that would have enough room for compassion and consideration.

His mother set the first examples of care, concern and simple living for her young son to follow. If she did not let anyone go away from her house without a meal, she practised equality in its most pristine form. Born around 1900 and living through some of the cruellest periods of caste-driven social segregation, she never believed that people could be untouchables, the lowliest segment in the Hindu caste hierarchy. Brahmins, Kshatriyas and Vaishyas would not let even the shadow of an untouchable cross their paths.

But Gouri Kunjamma could never understand how one human being could be inferior or superior to another, and while the untouchables worked outside her home, generally in the gardens and fields the family owned, she would be the first to rush to their help in the event of death, disease or childbirth amongst them. She would give them medicines and food, and derive joy from their smiles.

Even when she was in hospital battling cancer, she looked after a young, destitute woman, also suffering from the same disease and left to die by her son. Forty years later, the woman met Gopalakrishnan and told him how his mother's affection had nursed her back from the brink. For a long, long time, Gouri Kunjamma's spirit lived in that woman.

Gopalakrishnan's mother was an exception in her family, a rarity in her society, who taught her children that only humanity and humility mattered. The man carries this legacy in letter and spirit, to use a cliché.

Here are two examples, just two, but they speak volumes. In the world we live in today that promotes and practises another kind of caste system based on wealth and professional status, Gopalakrishnan is comfortable asking his cab driver to join him for lunch. He is equally at ease queuing up at a bank counter to buy a demand draft. One national newspaper photographer spotted him in one such queue in Chennai, and the picture was front-paged!

Often, humility in India is viewed as a sign of weakness, even cowardice. But one needs tremendous self-confidence and courage to be humble. Gopalakrishnan is an embodiment of these.

4

A Struggle Named School

Adoor once had to take an early morning flight out of Chennai, as, I am sure, he has had to on many occasions, and from many other cities. The plane was leaving at six, and Gopalakrishnan told me that he would have to wake up a good two hours or maybe three before the reporting time at the airport. He takes a while to get out of sleep mode. I suppose he is a night person, but early in his life this caused problems. Having gone to bed late, he would invariably get up late in the morning, his schoolmate-cousins, impatiently urging him to get a move on. He rues that he had to finish his morning tasks in just fifteen minutes. The school in this case, Adoor High School, was a good nine kilometres from home, the distance adding to his woes.

But Gopalakrishnan's first school, Kottara Government Primary School, was a mere furlong away from his home at Adoor. Once called Hindu Mission School, it was established by his family, more precisely his maternal uncles. However, by the time he joined the institution, it had been handed over to the government. 'So I studied in a government school,' Adoor says, and years later, he wanted his daughter Aswati, his only child, to go to a government school as well. But he was talked out of this by friends, who felt that times had changed, and government educational institutions were hopelessly inadequate to meet the challenges of the modern day. The friends felt that a bright student like Aswati would be handicapped if she were to pass through a government school. They were right, and today she is one of the country's finest police officers.

The Kottara school was a small affair with a big hall that was inventively divided into four classes, the institution having just up to the fourth grade. The benches were so arranged to create four imaginary rooms and segregate the students, a scene reminiscent of the Danish director Lars Von Trier's *Dogville* (2003), the set of the 1930s American town entirely built on a sound stage with marks on the floor indicating houses, street names, workplaces and so on.

At the Kottara school, there were not even screens to partition the classes, and the cacophony of voices that arose from the four teachers talking at the same time and on top of their voices made a strange scene. The students in each class— perched on benches with no desks, and usually armed with slates and pencils, not really books—had to concentrate hard to catch what their teacher was teaching. This was a great training for the children, who learnt the art of selective attention by ignoring the goings-on elsewhere in the hall. But was Gopalakrishnan himself equipped to do this? One is not sure, given the poor grades he got, and consistently so.

Though he enjoyed school in parts, he remembers that it was a struggle. At the primary level, he scored miserable marks, often single digits. The boy was just not interested in his textbooks. 'Probably I was very lazy, and I certainly never paid attention to what my teachers taught,' Adoor looks back on a time that was often torturous.

His teachers and parents sadly concluded that he was a failure. Writing him off, they labelled him *mandan* (dud), but this did not unduly worry him—rather it made him happy—because he saw the brighter side of it. Nobody would expect a *mandan* to perform, and perform well at that.

But he always managed to pass. He was never kept back, although he did not really deserve to be promoted. The school's headmaster was close to Gopalakrishnan's family. There was no question then of detaining him in a class. That would be sacrilege or almost, for after all the school owed its origin to the Mouttathu clan, and the headmaster his job.

Gopalakrishnan might have carried on the same way had it not gradually occurred to him that he was getting bored, even a little angry, with being seen as 'no good'. So, he decided to correct himself. 'I started to take my studies seriously when I was in the Vadakkedathukaavu Middle School, close to Adoor. Through sheer effort, I improved my percentages and rose to the top of the class. I had only one contender for the first rank. She was Susan Chacko, and I greatly admired her intelligence,' Adoor smiles.

He was better than Susan in the languages and every other subject, but not in mathematics. He could never figure out numbers, and those seemingly simple multiplications and additions were causing all the minuses in his mark-sheets, frustrating his efforts to beat the girl. Why Susan, of course.

When he entered the Adoor High School, he knew he would not get through his school-leaving examination unless he got a grip on mathematics. Appukkutan Nair was a good student. A friend of Gopalakrishnan, though older to him by a few years, Appukkutan offered help just as the examination was approaching, and showed his distraught young friend the steps to solve seemingly forbidding mathematical problems. In time, the puzzles of arithmetic and algebra no longer seemed as puzzling as before, and believe it or not, he passed his final school examination with 76 per cent in mathematics.

Appukkutan, Adoor regrets, did not go far in life. He dropped out of school, his brilliance all wasted. 'He could have been a great mathematics professor,' Adoor is sad that men such as Appukkutan do not get an opportunity to rise in life and serve society. They fall by the wayside. 'This is so unfair.'

There was another gifted student in school, in Gopalakrishnan's class, called Raghavan Kurup. He was also a genius in numbers, but later when Gopalakrishnan was in college at Pandalam, a town near Adoor, he saw in his cousin's field Raghavan tilling the land. When he walked up to Gopalakrishnan and greeted him, he felt quite awkward. 'As students we were equals, but later one faces a situation where one's classmate is no more than a coolie,' Adoor looks clearly upset. Years after that meeting on the farm, he is still not reconciled to the idea of inequality and injustice. Worse, he is even now troubled by the fact that he could do nothing to help Raghavan.

Times were bad then even for Gopalakrishnan. He was finding it hard to pay his tuition fee, which he had to once he got into middle school. The fee was small, but still difficult to shell out, because cash was not easy to come by, the economy being driven by paddy. Payments were made in grains.

And grains were not coming in either. Having rented out her rice fields to farmers and middlemen because there was no man to look after the farming, Gouri Kunjamma was invariably cheated by them with sob stories of crop failure and poor produce. But she somehow managed to find the fee money, and Gopalakrishnan passed through the portals of school and into college.

Raghavan could not, Appukkutan could not. But Susan could. Years later, Gopalakrishnan learnt from her younger sister that Susan was a professor in Germany and married a German.

College began with a scare for Gopalakrishnan. Uncle Gopalan Unnithan took the boy to the NSS College at Pandalam for his admission to what was then known as Intermediate, akin to the more recent Pre-University and the current Plus-

Two course. Principal Rama Iyer was impressed by the boy's mathematics marks, and the country had not yet seen such high figures like 98 and 99 per cent that students today aim at and even score. Iyer graciously offered Gopalakrishnan the top group, pure mathematics, a prized subject that students craved for. But the lad shuddered. He could not imagine going back to numbers, back to that agonizing struggle.

Iyer was a terror, and none dared to disagree with him. 'Let him take the first group so that he can become an engineer,' Iyer had said with an air of finality. The young Gopalakrishnan convinced his uncle later that he would like to take the second group, and I suppose Gopalan Unnithan agreed thinking that the boy would become a medical doctor.

He did become one, though with a difference, feeling the pulse of the people, and injecting them with thought-provoking entertainment. His stories stir souls, elevating moods to a new high. His film *Naalu Pennungal* was a hit in Kerala, and I saw audiences give an ovation at the end of a screening, something rarely seen in a commercial show. This was repeated after every screening. Even at Toronto, London, Rotterdam, Warsaw and Nantes, reports said that the people simply loved *Naalu Pennungal*.

Gopalakrishnan scored high marks in Intermediate Malayalam, proving that he was as good as an accomplished writer in the language. So he thought of doing a Bachelor's degree with honours in Malayalam, but was quickly dissuaded by his relatives, who did not want him to become a Malayalam teacher, a profession that was considered neither paying nor prestigious. Gopalakrishnan settled for zoology, and everybody thought that this was it. The route to a white coat.

Two months into his zoology classes, he saw an advertisement calling students to the Gandhigram Rural Institute, near Madurai and Dindigul in Tamil Nadu. Later, it became a university, and Gopalakrishnan, who had always been moved by Mahatma Gandhi's teachings, decided to give up zoology, pack his bags and travel to Gandhigram. For all those, including his guardian uncle, who were disappointed that he would not become a medical practitioner, he had a smart retort. 'What would I have done had I become a doctor? Obviously saved lives. I have done that now as well. Can you imagine the number of frogs, geckos and cockroaches I would have dissected and killed in my science laboratory?' Adoor's eyes light up.

He abhors the idea of killing. I remember an evening at Darsanam, when a civet that had made a home for itself and its family just above the wooden roof of his study eased itself, the urine dripping on his table crowded with books and documents. 'It is very difficult to drive them away, and I do not want to kill them,' Adoor tells me about his helplessness. However, the next minute he sounds cheerful when he says that the elder civets behave themselves. It is only the younger ones that cause this mischief. They are probably not yet toilet trained. His sense of humour does not desert him even in moments like this.

At Gandhigram (1957 to 1960), he took up public administration, economics and political science. But it was not the subjects and texts that excited the 18-year-old teenager, rather the new vistas that opened up for him there. It was the first time that he was seeing the sky in all its glorious vastness. 'In Kerala, the foliage is so thick that you can hardly see the sky,' Adoor on his first impressions of the Gandhigram skyline. Much like the sky that was independent of the earth, he was beginning to experience a new kind of freedom. He was staying away from home for the first time, away from the restrictive confines of a conservative community. Gandhigram offered a refreshingly different environment where Gopalakrishnan and others could develop as individuals, pursuing not so much their ambitions as their passions.

5

Enter, Play

Theatre fascinated Gopalakrishnan. At eight, he was on stage. At ten, he wrote his first play *Kapatayogi* (The Fake Yogi). So enamoured of theatre was he that much later when he went to the Pune Film Institute, he spent the first year reading plays, literally soaking himself in them. So what if he had gone there to study screenplay writing and direction. 'I thought a course in screenplay writing would help me become a professional playwright,' Adoor laughs at his early naivety.

Yet, when he began to make feature films in the early 1970s, his cinema emerged as pure cinema: minimalist, utterly visual and not at all verbose. He packed—and still does—sheer power in his frames, often so very sparse. I have always wondered how he managed to produce a work of this kind, given his own beginnings that were firmly rooted in a Kathakali culture, and India's brand of celluloid that grew out of theatre, not photography, as with the West. While the West pushed pictures into motion and movement (remember the American term for a movie was motion picture or just pictures), India made its first films out of theatrical plays.

During the closing years of the 1800s, Bengali photographer Hiralal Sen would place a camera in front of the stage and record scenes from dramas—the musical extravaganza, *Alibaba*, was one among the many—at Kolkata's (then Calcutta) famed Classic Theatre. These movies were screened after stage shows, and the experience of seeing a play playing on the screen was mesmeric.

Sometimes, the films were taken to remote areas where theatre actors found it difficult to travel or camp. The possibility of reaching out to large audiences through such images seemed immense, and the first decade of the twentieth century saw a phenomenal growth of this kind of cinema. It was highly overstated, but of course, for after all it was theatre where performers had to be loud and freely use their limbs. It was pure theatre, but on screen. Even today, some Indian movies are stagy, the theatrical tradition lingering on.

Gopalakrishnan's early zeal for theatre could have developed out of his family's love, respect and support for Kathakali. His grandfathers and uncles had troupes at home. The artists wore high-quality headgear made out of insect shells like those of blue-beetles. The headgear glowed brilliantly in the light of the lamp, and he still remembers labourers going out into the fields and forests to trap blue-beetles every time a new one had to be made. Renowned Kathakali performers, such as Kalamandalam Krishnan Nair, would often insist on borrowing the headgear Gopalakrishnan's family had in its treasured collections. Today, gilt paper is used, not insect shells.

His earliest memory of Kathakali is perhaps of brightly painted faces, puffed up costumes and men with slow, deliberate, stylized action enacting a story with rhythmic eye movements and arm gesticulations. Secure in his mother's lap, he would watch a presentation, perhaps wide-eyed, and listen to her as she explained to the women sitting around her what was happening on the stage. The little lad must have imbibed and retained a lot of this drama.

For, as Chidananda Das Gupta, cinema critic and director, writes in his latest book, *Seeing is Believing*, 'Adoor's work shows an affinity to Kathakali's extreme formality of style. Kathakali's totally reconstructed image of the human figure when he appears on the stage, with the face painted in emphatic colours and the body draped in innumerable angles and folds of cloth that hide his form, make him only a Kathakali artist. It is through this complex cloak of artifice that one has to recognize a character in a Kathakali performance. The individual human being is wiped out; a character in the play possesses him, inhabits his body . . . It is tempting to think that Adoor's work has a similar dimension of masking reality behind artifice, challenging the audience to discover what it may.' The movements of some of Gopalakrishnan's actors are 'slow, deliberate and stylistic,' Das Gupta comments. 'And consistent with this theatre background is the fact that Adoor uses camera movements very sparingly; the bedrock of his filming is the steady shot more often than not at eye level.'

In an interview to *Asian Cinema* in 1997, Adoor agreed, though not with certainty, that 'maybe my background in Kathakali has influenced my work. Maybe. I am not sure . . .' Adoor also agreed with the interviewer, Suranjan Ganguly, that his cinema may feel like a 'Kathakali performance', but the style of acting does not resemble the style of the dance-theatre. 'Realism is my source material, my springboard. It creates the authenticity of what you see.'

Yet, Ganguly felt that there was more than 'just a conceptual relationship between Adoor's cinema and Kathakali. The visual style seems to draw on some of its conventions as well—how he stages the action, groups his characters, uses a black background out of which his characters often emerge.'

Adoor tells me after much pondering that Kathakali has become a part of his culture, his way of living. Perhaps so much so, as I feel, that he does not even realize the theatre's impact on his life and work.

'Kathakali engrosses me completely,' Adoor told *Deep Focus* magazine in an interview in 2001. 'While watching a performance, I forget everything else—the external world, all the personal problems ... There is hardly anything in it that relates to the present and there is no effort at being realistic. I think the percussion and the ambience as a whole transport us completely to a different world. And it has always been such a creative stimulus for me. Here each role is being defined anew by actors each time they perform it. Now Kalamandalam Gopi is defining how Nalan [the prince in *Nalacharitham* in the Indian epic, Mahabharata] should be. Earlier it was Kalamandalam Krishnan Nair. Tomorrow it will be somebody else. It keeps on changing and evolving.'

This is the greatness of Kathakali. Nothing is created to last or to be preserved. Every creation is for that evening. The day after will see another creation. The day after that, yet another.

But sadly Kathakali and other Kerala art forms were considered worthless when Gopalakrishnan was growing up. What was cherished and sought after was Western theatre. 'So we spent our time reading, studying, writing and producing such plays. We were always looking West. I feel it was a great loss. It was thrust upon us that proper theatre should have unity of space and time. And we were totally convinced of that, no doubts or hesitations here. So Kathakali did not mean much to us. We had acquired different yardsticks of quality judgment, and these arts like Kathakali questioned such rigid conceptions of space and time,' Adoor said in the same *Deep Focus* interview.

Though he made splendid documentaries on Kathakali artists—Guru Chenganoor, Kalamandalam Gopi (1999) and Kalamandalam Ramankutty Nair (2005)—he was not greatly attracted to this form of entertainment in his younger days, when life was a play, sheer play. At eight, he was Siddharta— the ancient Indian prince who renounced pleasure and left his beautiful wife, Yasodara, and baby son, Rahul, to find the meaning of life. Siddharta eventually found Buddhism. Before he attained enlightenment under a bodhi tree at Bodh Gaya in Bihar and became the Buddha or the Enlightened One, he was the Prince of Kapilavastu, now part of Nepal.

It is the prince that Gopalakrishnan essayed on stage. Even today, he does not know why his schoolteacher, who penned the play, chose him. 'At that age, one does not show any histrionic talent. Maybe I was smarter than the rest of the students. I do not know the reason.' His elder sisters presented him with new clothes and shoes, befitting of the royal prince. 'I was all set to show off my costume,' he laughs. But his joy was short-lived. A cousin of his in his class, more influential than little Gopalakrishnan, protested. Or, rather his parents did. They must have complained to the teacher saying that their son had no role at all in the play. So the part was divided into two. The first dealt with the prince and his rich life with all the trappings of royalty, replete with fine clothes. The second traced his disillusionment with all this finery and superficiality, and his abandonment of the palace. He walks out one night dressed in just a loin cloth.

Gopalakrishnan was asked to play the disenchanted Siddharta, and what a blow it was to the lad. 'I was heartbroken,' he says, 'because I could not wear my new clothes and shoes and go on stage.' But the teacher's word was law and his decision final. The play was part of the Travancore maharaja Sree Chithira Thirunal's birthday celebrations, and everybody from Gopalakrishnan's house, including uncles and aunts, watched him as he dramatized the role without any fright. It was incredible for an eight-year-old to be so bold in a hall full of people.

That evening, he was applauded and recognized as an actor. Later, he invariably did female parts. In those days, girls never acted and amateur theatre had men playing women. Often, Gopalakrishnan was the heroine, much to the chagrin of his sisters, whose saris he borrowed and messed up. However, in the plays he wrote, he portrayed the male lead. Here, he could cast the actors. And himself too—as the hero!

He loved this new role, of writing and acting out plays. And he had company. Two cousins, almost as old as he, were his great friends. I suppose friendship among cousins and other relatives was common then, given the limited opportunity children had of meeting anybody outside their own families. Even in school, many children belonged to Gopalakrishnan's clan. So insular was that society.

The three cousins—Ravindran, Narayanan and Gopalakrishnan, nicknamed RNG Company—met every Sunday and on other holidays usually in a cashew grove. Each, armed with a notebook and pencil, would climb atop a tree, put on his thinking cap and write his very own masterpiece. At lunch, they would get down, compare notes and critically analyse one another's writings that varied from poetry to short story to drama.

On special occasions, usually at festivals such as Onam (celebrated every August or September during harvest in Kerala) and Shivarathri (falls usually every February or March, when devotees spend the night chanting the name of Shiva), the RNG would put up plays at Gopalakrishnan's house. There was a lot of freedom there, since there was no man around. His father was usually at work in some distant forest.

It was not only plays that the boys organized. There was great variety. Solo acting and music recitals added to the richness of the programme and made the evening truly delightful. What is more, the RNG got a decent audience. Men, women and even the elderly came to watch them, and Adoor tells me that he and his cousins were taken seriously by adults. To Adoor 'it was a real, genuine presentation of theatre', and quite modern in a sense. There were no props, no curtains. There was an instance, he remembers, of his younger brother essaying a character who dies. There was no way he could be covered, and so he just got up and walked away. That was it.

In some ways, Gopalakrishnan was lucky enough to be associated with people who also shared his interest. In his middle school days, there was a drawing teacher, who was a playwright of sorts. He would present his work in the school, and he found Gopalakrishnan an ideal actor. Rather an ideal actress! Once again, the boy found himself playing women. 'And I had no choice,' Adoor says, 'because without me, the plays could not be presented. Nobody else fit the bill.'

His school days were also a time of vibrant theatre movement in India that began some years earlier. In 1943, the Indian People's Theatre Association was formed in Mumbai (then Bombay); interestingly at the same time the Communist Party of India was holding its first congress in the city. Sitar maestro Ravi Shankar, actors Utpal Dutt and Balraj Sahni, cinema directors Ritwik Ghatak and Khwaja Ahmad Abbas and poet Kaifi Azmi led the association, and liberally borrowing from traditional and folk art forms they produced plays critiquing imperialism and fascism.

Seven years later, the Kerala People's Arts Club was born. It became a force to reckon with on the Kerala's cultural scene with its play, *Ningalenne Communistakki* (You Made Me a Communist) by Thoppil Bhasi. The club had definite political and social messages to convey.

The theatre scene in Kerala then was pulsating with the plays of N. Krishna Pillai, C.J. Thomas, Ponkunnam Varkey, K.T. Mohammed and others. They dealt with social and psychological themes that marked the beginnings of modern Kerala theatre.

All this inspired Gopalakrishnan, and it inspired him deeply. He was sure that his career would be in theatre. 'This was going to be my field, whether I work in an office or elsewhere,' Adoor's mind was made up. So he kept acting all through school and college, and penning plays, sometimes winning prizes.

It was at Gandhigram that he began reading plays in

English. Till then it had been in Malayalam. He read all the important ones published in English, and also extensively about the playwrights—John Galsworthy, Henrik Ibsen, Luigi Pirandello, Tennesee Williams, Thornton Wilder, Harold Pinter and Bertolt Brecht among others. He perused the entire works of George Bernard Shaw—some fifty-odd plays—the Irish writer, whose intellectualism and humour were unmatched among his contemporaries.

Gopalakrishnan's wit is as endearing, and I have seen him crack a joke even in the face of adversity. Men like Shaw probably moulded his thinking and outlook, and Gopalakrishnan took pains to understand them.

Coming from a community where people spoke mostly in Malayalam, his English vocabulary was severely limited. So he kept a dictionary by his side, referring to it ever so often, and to make all this comfortable, nay enjoyable, he had a special chair made at home and taken to Gandhigram. The chair had a broad hand-rest that could hold a dictionary and a notebook as well!

Perched on this chair, tucked away in a corner and lost, lost to the world, he tackled the entire corpus of Shaw, all his plays, at one go, and even the introductions, some of which were longer than the plays themselves, like in the case of *Back to Methuselah*. 'I was genuinely interested in theatre,' Adoor explains why he made such an effort to comprehend Shaw and others.

And when an important Malayalam playwright, G. Sankara Pillai, joined Gandhigram as a teacher, it came as a boon to the teenager thirsting for theatre, and more of it. 'The writer became a model for me,' Adoor's eyes light up. Pillai had just then begun writing some of his most outstanding works that made him a revered figure in Kerala. It must have made Gopalakrishnan extremely proud when Pillai gave him his manuscripts to read and comment on. Pillai also added to the Gandhigram library, stocking it up with innumerable books on plays, playwriting and production. Later in 1977, he set up the School of Drama in Calicut University. Unfortunately, he died young, at sixty.

And Gopalakrishnan was reading all that Pillai had collected and acquired for Gandhigram. This meant he had less time to write his own plays, and the number came down to barely one or two a year during his three years there.

A play that he wrote and still remembers very well was called *Aniyara* (The Green Room), which won the best prize at a theatre festival. About an amateur group preparing to produce a play, it fizzles out in the green room, even before the curtain goes up. The concept was novel, and the theme caught on. A couple of his other dramatic works, *Ninte Rajyam Varunnu* (Thy Kingdom Cometh) and *Vaiki Vanna Velicham* (The Light that Came Late) were published.

Later, when he was working in Thiruvananthapuram as a statistical investigator in the National Sample Survey, he staged a few plays. He continued doing so even later—till 1974, the year when he put up Samuel Beckett's *Waiting for Godot* in Malayalam. This was his last stage production. By then he had made his first celluloid feature, *Swayamvaram*. I suppose even at that point in time, his heart was in theatre. His first love, really. And it must have taken him quite an attempt to pull himself completely away from it.

For him, life had certainly been a drama (it still is), and his world, a stage. People made their entries and their exits while Gopalakrishnan stood by watching them. He thought about them, analysed them. Some were monsters. Some angels. And some were men, just men. And he created out of them unforgettable characters, such as Vishwanathan in *Swayamvaram*, Sankarankutty in *Kodiyettam*, Unni in *Elippathayam*, Sreedharan in *Mukhamukham*, Ajayan in *Anantaram*, Bhaskara Patelar in *Vidheyan* and Kaliyappan in *Nizhalkkuthu*.

6

Spinning Wonders and Woes

There was spring in the air, and the evening was pleasant. Mahatma Gandhi, helped by two girls, walked across the lawns of New Delhi's Birla House for his evening prayer meeting. As he climbed the steps leading to the terrace at the end of the lawns, Nathuram Godse, a fanatic Hindu, emptied several bullets into the frail frame of Gandhi. That day, 30 January 1948, the world lost one of the greatest apostles of peace.

Nobody is sure whether he uttered 'Hey Ram' as he collapsed, but the man, whom everybody called Mahatma, fell prey to violence and vindictiveness, hatred and malice. All his life he fought these evils.

In Adoor, far, far away from the blood-soaked steps of New Delhi's Birla House, a boy, around seven, sobbed when his family broke the news of Gandhi's death. This has been recreated in *Kathapurushan*, with all its poignancy. Gopalakrishnan wept the whole evening. Nobody could console him. In some vague way he could understand that a great man had been killed, and he was upset about it.

That day, Gopalakrishnan became a Gandhian. It may not have been apparent then, but later at school, as early as that, he spun the charka and wore khadi. He still wears them, and the charka continues to be part of his life and work.

When he was shooting *Nizhalkkuthu* on the Kerala–Tamil Nadu border, he needed a charka and went looking for one. But he just could not find it. Later, he was told that the Tamils called it rattu. And rattu he found easily. The one that the hangman Kaliyappan's son uses in the film now adorns Darsanam along with the bullock cart, also used in the same movie.

Nizhalkkuthu strongly reflects Gandhian values. A powerful indictment of capital punishment, the work shows in an ironical twist how the son—who spins the charka and follows Gandhi, even taking an active part in his freedom movement—is forced to step into his father's shoes and carry out an execution when the old man falls ill just before the hanging. Gandhian philosophy abounds even in *Kathapurushan*.

There is a lot of Gandhi in Gopalakrishnan. Even today, he likes to do his own work, instead of asking others. 'Maybe I owe it to Gandhi, who taught us the dignity of work, any work,' Adoor says. 'I enjoy this.' His cinematographer, Mankada Ravi Varma, who shot nine of his eleven films right from *Swayamvaram* to *Nizhalkkuthu*, once observed that his director did just about everything himself on the set. He never ordered others. This is obvious even outside the set. He never asks anybody to do anything he himself can.

At school, he began to wear khadi and study Hindi. The Hindi Prachar Sabha conducted courses in the language, and he passed the Madhyam examination. Gandhi evoked an abiding national feeling in young Gopalakrishnan, a sentiment that pushed him to join the Gandhigram Rural Institute in 1957, a year after it opened.

The name of the institute certainly caught Gopalakrishnan's attention, maybe his fancy too. It was preparing young people for social work, and the first two decades of India's independence were marked by intense patriotic fervour when cinema and theatre promoted Gandhian thinking and Nehruvian idealism. Raj Kapoor made movies on these early in his career. So did many others. Gopalakrishnan's first work, *Swayamvaram*, was an affirmation of Gandhi's beliefs. One of them was an individual's right to make his or her own choices: we see Sita and Viswanathan deciding to live together against parental wish. *One's Own Choice* was what it was about.

Gandhigram, which was a residential institute, greatly appealed to Gopalakrishnan. Nestled in a valley among Tamil Nadu's Sirumalai Hills, the home of nutritious *malaipazham* (hill banana), Gandhigram was a mix of many things. To begin with, it was unconventional. It was started by two close disciples of Gandhi, G. Ramachandran and his wife, T.S. Soundram.

Soundram was born in 1904 to the hard-working and legendary industrialist T.V. Sundaram Iyengar and Lakshmi Ammaiyar. A bright and courageous girl, she was always keen on helping those less privileged than her. Married during her early teens to Soundararajan, she was widowed in 1925. She was just twenty-one, and Indian society shunned and segregated widows. Her husband, a medical doctor, died of plague during an epidemic in Madurai. One of his last wishes was to see Soundram as a physician and wife again. He did not want her to remain a widow and lead an oppressed life, adhering to age-old restrictive customs.

Soundram agreed, walked away from blind, meaningless social norms, went back to school and then to medical college. Eleven years after her husband died, she graduated in medicine, even as she was in the thick of Gandhi's freedom struggle. It was during her college days in Delhi that she met Ramachandran. He was involved in Gandhi's Harijan (Children of God, a name given to untouchables by Gandhi) movement. He had been a student at Rabindranath Tagore's Visva-Bharati

University in Shantiniketan, West Bengal, and the friendship between Soundram and Ramachandran was bonded by their mutual concern for the exploited masses.

Defying parental opposition, the two married in 1940, a union blessed by Gandhi, who spun a mangal-sutra (a chain that a Hindu woman wears around her neck after marriage) and dipped it in turmeric, considered an auspicious practice. He believed inter-caste or inter-religious or inter-language marriages would promote the country's integration and national unity. His son, Devdas, married C. Rajagopalachari's (who was the second Governor-General of independent India and later the Chief Minister of Madras State, now called Tamil Nadu) daughter, Lakshmi. Soundram was a Tamil Iyengar, and Ramachandran a Malayalee Nair. And Gandhigram borrowed from Tagore and Gandhi—Ramachandran having lived in the latter's Sevagram Ashram for some time.

This was Gandhigram, where many interesting things happened. 'In the morning, we were all engaged in cleaning the place—the streets, buildings and residential houses. After a bath, we would all assemble at a large prayer hall, where passages from the Gita, the Quran and the Bible would be read,' Adoor remembers his days at Gandhigram. 'Sometimes, even verses from the Tamil epic *Thirukkural* would be recited. This would be followed by Ramachandran's lecture on world affairs and Soundram's on health, hygiene and so on'.

What was even more attractive to Gopalakrishnan were the talks by visiting dignitaries, such as Jawaharlal Nehru (independent India's first Prime Minister), Sarvepalli Radhakrishnan (independent India's second President) and Martin Luther King Jr (Afro-American civil rights leader). It was a great time at Gandhigram, where Gopalakrishnan and others learnt about India, its priorities, its dreams and its distresses, spinning both wonders and woes on their wheels of imagination.

But not everything was hunky-dory at Gandhigram, and

Gopalakrishnan was slowly overcome by disillusionment. 'After a while, I did not like the way Gandhian ideology was being practised. The principles were getting fossilized. They were becoming sheer rituals, without soul and meaning. And to my horror, I found most teachers at Gandhigram had their children studying in elite public schools in Madurai and elsewhere.' Adoor was clearly unhappy.

So were other students, who gradually became critical, and openly so, of this duplicity in standards. Adoor quotes the famous Polish film-maker Krzysztof Zanussi to make this point: 'Socialism is for the neighbour, not for us.' So it was for Gandhism at Gandhigram.

A website biography of Zanussi has this to say: 'His concern with the conflict between public and private morality, official corruption and the delicate balance between intellect and intuition are further explored in *A Woman's Decision* (1977), *Camouflage* (1977), and *Spirale/Spiral/Quarterly Balance* (1978). In a cameo appearance as himself in (another Polish helmer) Krzysztof Kieslowski's *Camera Buff* (1979), Zanussi expresses his interest in the workings of corruption and compromise. This philosophical and moral dilemma is fully explored in *Ways in the Night* (1979), in which a basically decent German officer is called on to uphold the policies of National Socialism, and in the splendid *The Constant Factor* (1980). One of Zanussi's finest films, *The Constant Factor* further complicates the moral issues by the workings of chance: the young protagonist loses his opportunities for a successful career because of his refusal to compromise his ideals, only to become the unwitting cause of a tragedy.'

Later, Zanussi became a critic of socialism.

As did many students at Gandhigram of Gandhism. Gopalakrishnan too, although his mild manners, I would suppose, never gave room for anything vociferous or overt.

It was during his days at Gandhigram that his mother was diagnosed with cancer and had to be hospitalized in

Thiruvananthapuram. Every weekend and holiday, he would take a train from Chinnalapatti (the closest train station to Gandhigram and renowned for its brand of handloom sari) to Kerala to see his mother. She succumbed to the disease in 1962.

Before his mother fell ill, he would sometimes go home, where he would reassemble the same troupe that he used to work with, and present amateur plays. He does not remember what those plays were.

He has other anecdotes about Gandhigram. Once, a professor took students to Chennai (then Madras), and they had a *jatka* (horse-drawn cart) ride from Thiruvelikeni (Triplicane then) to the movie studios at Kodambakkam, a long journey indeed. At Bharani Studio, they watched the shoot of *Veera Pandiya Kattabomman* (an eighteenth-century Indian Tamil freedom fighter). 'I saw Sivaji Ganesan and Manorama on the set,' Adoor remembers the day quite clearly. It was a hot afternoon in 1958. 'After every take, the actors would go rushing out, because it was very hot on the set. The speed of the film was so low those days that one needed many, many lights for correct exposure.'

Back in Gandhigram, Gopalakrishnan was exposed to cinema classics. His passion for theatre did offer a stiff resistance, though, for acquiring an interest in movies. But I think at some point the curiosity for a very young art form like cinema must have got the better of his old loyalty. And after all, the magic of motion and movement is too hard to resist.

He remembers watching Satyajit Ray's first feature in Bengali, *Pather Panchali* (Song of the Little Road, 1955), in 1958. It was a 16-mm print and had no subtitles. Completed over a three-year period at great hardship with Ray even having to pawn his wife Bijoya's jewellery—the movie though winning only a minor prize at the 1956 Cannes Film Festival, Best Human Document, floored the world, and Gopalakrishnan.

To quote Lindsay Anderson in *The Observer*, 'You cannot

make films like this in a studio nor for money. Satyajit Ray has worked with humility and complete dedication; he has gone down on his knees in the dust. And his film has the quality of intimate, unforgettable experience.'

Thus began a sequence of events that was to place Ray almost at once among the great directors of the world— launching his extraordinary career. *Pather Panchali* put India on the world cinema map.

Adoor tells me that he loved *Pather Panchali* 'for strange reasons ... nobody was made up. I liked it, the idea of real people. And I liked the old people with so many wrinkles on their faces. I liked that. The Bengal village looked similar to ones in Kerala. So, I was trying to draw parallels between the movie and my own experiences. This is how you always relate. I found the scenes of the kitten and sweetmeat very interesting. But there was one big problem: the characters talked, and in the absence of subtitles I could not make out what they were saying. So, the story was not quite clear to me. Yet, I liked the work.'

It would be wrong to assume that Gopalakrishnan fell in love with cinema after *Pather Panchali*. He says that the medium was still, even at that stage, very distant to him. He had very little idea about it, and never imagined then that someday he would be working in it. 'Even when I saw a film, which was not often, I looked at it from a distance. There was no reason for me to get close to it because my basic interest was theatre.'

Yet, when he began to make movies, he never made one that was theatrical or loud. 'That is true because it is very important to know what theatre is to avoid duplicating it on screen,' Adoor's explanation is incisive.

After passing out of Gandhigram in 1960, he began to look for a job. Uncle Gopalan Unnithan had been taking care of him, and his young nephew did not want to burden him any longer. He went to Gwalior in Madhya Pradesh for an interview at the Agriculture University, which required an investigator. Gopalakrishnan knew Hindi and was very well qualified for the assignment. Yet, he did not get it, because his interviewers asked him questions in some strange language or dialect that was certainly not Hindi. Obviously, they did not want someone from outside their state to join the university.

This was the second time in his life he had failed an interview. Earlier, when he was at high school, he sought an apprenticeship in the boys' merchant navy. The requirements were simple: one had to be between twelve and fourteen years of age and should have passed the seventh standard. 'My mother was going through financial problems and I thought that I must help her. So I went to Thiruvananthapuram with her permission for an interview. But the navy rejected me. I was heartbroken, because I had gone there with the high expectation of being able to earn a stipend of thirty or forty rupees a month. That was not to be,' Adoor on his tryst with the job market.

However, long after this, and soon after his Gwalior debacle, he applied for a position in Thiruvananthapuam's National Sample Survey, and got in despite stiff competition. The salary was good, much higher than that of his brother Ramachandran Unnithan, a college lecturer. 'I was very pleased that I could give some money to my mother every month. Not because she needed it at that time, but it was my wish,' Adoor on his desire to make his mother happy.

For a year and a half, he worked there, but was somehow never quite happy. 'In the end, I was totally demoralized, because however sincerely you may work, your boss will always find some fault or the other with you. Finally, I could not take it any longer,' Adoor talks of his professional frustration.

There was something else that rankled him. Gopalan Unnithan suffered a stroke the night before Gopalakrishnan was to have met him and broken the news of his first job at the National

Sample Survey. He may not have been superstitious, but he felt uncomfortable that a man he loved and respected and who had been his guardian should have passed away before Gopalakrishnan could give him what then seemed such a great piece of news: being employed for the first time.

In any case, he was clearly unhappy with the National Sample Survey, and when he came across an advertisement in 1961 calling students to the Pune Film Institute (television had not become part of it), he applied for the 1962 course in screenplay writing and direction. And was selected. For several months before Gopalakrishnan saw the advertisement, he had been toying with the idea of getting into New Delhi's National School of Drama. But he hesitated, because he knew his Hindi was not good enough. The last thing he wanted again was a replay of the Gwalior interview. It had been awfully humiliating for him, and he was still smarting from that.

So, Pune it was. Destiny was probably pushing the young man towards cinematic adventure.

7

Days and Nights in Pune

Yet, Pune almost did not happen. The minimum qualification needed to join the film institute was a bachelor's degree. Gopalakrishnan did not have one, although he had a diploma from Gandhigram that was equivalent to a bachelor's degree with honours. 'I wrote to the institute saying that I had a letter from the Central Ministry of Education that said this. In fact, at Gandhigram, I studied advanced economics and politics, and I was more than qualified to join Pune,' Adoor talks about those days of anticipation and anguish.

The institute relented, and admitted him, though provisionally. Eventually, the ministry sent a clarification to the institute, and he got in. Had the institute gone by the book, an extremely bright student would have missed an opportunity to learn cinema from some of the greatest teachers of the time. And who knows, he may have never made movies, such engaging movies at that.

Gandhigram later became a university, and in 2006, when it was celebrating its golden jubilee, it honoured Gopalakrishnan as one of its most distinguished alumni.

At Pune, he passed the written test and did extremely well in the following interview, conducted by Khwaja Ahmad Abbas (who penned neo-realist films, such as *Neecha Nagar/ Lower Depths*, *Awara/*Vagabond, *Saat Hindustani/*Seven Indians and *Naya Sansar/*New World, and was awarded the Padma Shri in 1969) and others. Gopalakrishnan was ranked number one and given a merit scholarship of Rs 75 a month, the only one that year to have been awarded this.

His understanding of plays and playwrights certainly endeared him to Abbas and his team of interviewers, and they were impressed by what he knew. Gopalakrishnan was the only one among the candidates to have published a few plays, and was well versed in both Malayalam and English literature. And it helped, at least in getting him the scholarship, meagre though it was. He was drawing a salary four times this amount at the National Sample Survey, but he quit that to pursue his passion.

He joined the screenplay writing and direction course at Pune in 1962, hoping to learn more about theatre. But instead he discovered cinema, which held him in a tight embrace, gradually weaning him away from the stage. 'I never imagined that I would be working in this medium some day,' Adoor smiles.

Theatre had been his life's ambition since schooldays, and even the choice of screenplay writing and direction at Pune was made on the belief that they would compliment his knowledge of theatre and give him a formal training in drama. He was completely mistaken. He soon came to realize that there were more differences than similarities between writing a stage play and a screenplay, he reminisces in *Cinema Anubhavam*.

But for one long year at Pune, he was reading about theatre, which was going through very exciting times then. New plays were being written, new playwrights emerging. It was the time when Samuel Beckett's *Waiting for Godot* and Harold Pinter's new works—*The Room*, *The Birthday Party* and *The*

Caretaker—were coming into India, and Gopalakrishnan read them all.

In the end, the lure of cinema proved irresistible, and when the second year of his course began, he was hooked to movies. He found that he had seen very few pictures till then, hardly any from Bollywood or Hollywood. He had never seen European cinema, and so he started in earnest to make up for the lost time. Pune's Alka screened Hollywood fare on Sunday mornings, and for half the usual admission rates. Some interesting films were produced in the 1950s and 1960s, and they all came quickly to India. There were no import restrictions then, and large companies such as Warner Brothers and Metro Goldwyn Mayer had their own theatres in India, and exhibited the movies they made. He simply adored *Come September* and *Roman Holiday.*

Some other theatres showed contemporary Hindi cinema on Sundays, and Gopalakrishnan feasted on this. These Sunday films were in addition to what he saw at the institute, and that was quite a spread as well. Bimal Roy, Guru Dutt and Raj Kapoor enchanted the twenty-something youth, and their early works were passionate, patriotic and pleasing. They made a kind of cinema that touched Gopalakrishnan's heart. His loyalty to the stage was being gradually eroded by his new-found love for the screen, a classic case of the mistress proving to be far more seductive than the wife. His teachers aided and abetted this affair!

'We had a remarkable professor called R.S. Pruthi, who asked us to write a screenplay every two weeks. He was strict, and we had to type the script and bind the pages before submitting it,' Adoor says. 'This created a problem. I had to get my manuscript typed by someone else, and it would come back to me with glaring errors. This is when I decided to buy a typewriter. With the money I got from the National Sample Survey, I bought myself a J.K. Typewriter and a guide by Pitman. I had never used a typewriter before, and knew nothing about it. But I learnt quickly. In about a week's time, I could type my manuscripts.'

Once he had mastered the keyboard, things became very simple. He had been penning plays since he was ten, and when Pruthi asked the class to write a screenplay from, let us say, a Tagore story, Gopalakrishnan did it in no time.

At the end of the second year, the class was told to write original stories, and in the final examination, Gopalakrishnan scored high marks, his background in theatre helping him enormously. Abbas was one of the examiners, and he liked Gopalakrishnan's work. He told Pruthi that if there were boys like Gopalakrishnan who wrote such good scripts, the course was well worth the effort.

Abbas must have been fond of the boy, for he followed his career. At the 1985 International Film Festival of India in New Delhi, where *Mukhamukham* was screened, it created a flutter. The Communists were angry that he should have made an 'anti-Communist' movie. At the press meet after the screening, Abbas came in a wheelchair, and despite being quite sick, gave moral support to his one-time favourite student.

Columns of criticism were written about *Mukhamukham*, and a lot of them panned the work. But Gopalakrishnan could not care less, and he dared to take on the holy cow of Communism in the very heart of the lion's den. Kerala, of course. That was Adoor, fearless enough to stand by his point of view. Ray described *Mukhamukham* as 'bold and courageous', and quipped, who would have ever thought of making a picture about a man who is always sleeping.

Besides Pruthi, there were other professors at Pune whom Gopalakrishnan admired. One of them was the Bengali film maverick Ritwik Ghatak. He became the institute's vice-principal and professor of direction in 1964 on Satyajit Ray's recommendation to Indira Gandhi, who was then the Minister for Information and Broadcasting in the Lal Bahadur Shastri Cabinet.

Mind you, the rumour then was that Ray and Ghatak were sworn enemies. Rumour it must have been, fanned and fuelled by people who either hated Ray or Ghatak. Ray once said that when he heard that Ghatak had died in a hospital, he went there to pay respects. When Ray came out of the hospital, a group of young men abused him. 'You killed Ghatak,' they had shouted.

But the fact is each had but admiration for the other. Ray once remarked: 'Ritwik was one of the few truly original talents in the cinema this country has produced ... As a creator of powerful images in an epic style he was virtually unsurpassed in Indian cinema. Had *Nagarik* [*The Citizen*, made in 1952, but opened in Kolkata's New Empire in 1977, a year after Ghatak's untimely death at age fifty] been released before my *Pather Panchali* [1955], *Nagarik* would have been accepted as the first film of the alternative form of Bengali cinema.'

I am sure Ray meant that. I had known him, being his son Sandip's classmate at Kolkata's St Xavier's College, where we graduated with political science. I still remember pushing the buzzer at Ray's flat on Kolkata's Bishop Lefroy Road, and the man himself would answer the door. Such was his humility. I have never found Ray petty or mean, and his professionalism and fondness for cinema could have never allowed him to harbour any malice towards Ghatak.

Ghatak's praise for Ray was as high. He once commented: 'It is true that *Pather Panchali* was based on a famous novel [by Bengali writer Bhibutibhushan Bandopadhyay]. But for the first time, a literary story was narrated in the filmic idiom. The language was sound. Artistic truth was upheld. The fundamental difference between the two art forms was delineated.'

Ghatak was a genius, and perhaps greater than Ray. But Ghatak's alcoholism and lack of discipline ruined his reputation and affected his work. Some would say that unlike Ghatak, Ray was in the right place at the right time. Maybe, but Ray's extraordinary ability to lead a regimented life was his scoring point.

Ghatak was a scholar: he was an expert in the Vedas. What is more, he was well versed in modern science and Western philosophy. 'This impressed us students in no small measure. Close friends knew that cinema and alcohol ran in Ghatak's veins. His enthusiasm for the medium was such that once he himself made a movie that a student of his was supposed to have as part of his curriculum. Ghatak was an outstanding film-maker and an innovative teacher,' Adoor comments in *Cinema Anubhavam.*

'Ten years after I had completed my Pune Institute course in 1965, I met Ghatak at a New Delhi seminar. It was a year before his untimely death. After the speeches had been delivered, I walked up to Ghatak and extending my hand asked him whether he remembered me. "No," he said. I tried hard to hide my embarrassment.' And perhaps disappointment.

It was at Pune that Gopalakrishnan learnt the alphabet of cinema technique. Ghatak screened his own movies and explained the various aspects in each frame. These classes proved to be the lessons of a lifetime for young Gopalakrishnan.

Ghatak also showed several clips from Ray's body of work, setting at rest, once and for all, the stories about enmity between these two giants. Gopalakrishnan saw much of the early Ray: *Aparajito* (The Unvanquished, 1956), *Parash Pathar* (The Philosopher's Stone, 1958), *Jalsaghar* (The Music Room, 1958), *Apur Sansar* (The World of Apu, 1959), *Devi* (The Goddess, 1960), *Teen Kanya* (Three Daughters, 1961), *Kanchenjungha* (1962), *Abhijan* (The Expedition, 1962), *Mahanagar* (The Big City, 1963) and *Charulata* (The Lonely Wife, 1964).

Apart from craft, students studied the history and growth of this fascinating new art form, its technological advancement and its aesthetics. They saw films made since the days of the Lumiere Brothers (their first 'moving images' were screened in

December 1895 in Paris), and how cinema evolved, each movie or a group of movies featuring a certain innovation or development. They also read about these.

Gopalakrishnan was almost spellbound by the enormous possibilities cinema offered. There was never anything like this before. Indeed. And he explored them, is still exploring them. 'As much as it offers, cinema also demands. It is a difficult mistress. There are a thousand ways camera lenses, for instance, can be used, but one must be able to make the right choices,' Adoor explains.

'But lenses are only one part of filming. There is camera movement, composition of a shot or sequence, the role of colour and so on. The camera must move in a way that audiences should not notice it, and there has got to be a good reason for the camera to shift. One must choreograph it in such a way that viewers do not see the movement,' Adoor lets us into some of his fantastic methods.

'Audiences want to know what is happening in a character's mind. They want to know how he or she is responding to a situation or development. So, you have to take these into account while filming a scene.

'As I was saying earlier, cinema is demanding because it is not just photography. It is not just composition, it is not just colours, it is not even just technology. It is not just sound and effects. But much more than all these,' says Adoor on what cinema is all about.

'Cinema is actually one's experience. One's vision of life. The film-maker's. That is his cinema. This is why, I feel, cinema is so demanding that one cannot have one's attention diverted or distracted.'

Pune helped him understand all this, realize the enormous potential of the medium. He was excited by motion and movement, and when he walked into the institute, he had not even touched a still camera, let alone taken a photograph. Professor G.B. Kulkarni taught cinematography, and his class began with a simple exercise. He gave his students a camera each, told them how it worked, asked them to go out and capture an image.

Armed with the camera, Gopalakrishnan went out like a boy on his first date. He had never before held a camera, though he had a bookish knowledge of it. He had no idea what to shoot. Not that he did not have a choice. It was a sunny day. Outside his classroom, there was a garden with flowers and butterflies, there was a road and there were buildings and people. Yet, he could not help feeling bewildered. He had no idea how to compose a shot. It was a real challenge. Finally, after hours of struggle, tempered by an inner debate, he clicked a picture. It had been difficult deciding what to freeze, and it had been even more difficult executing his decision. There was a water tank and a drainage cavity large enough for him to crawl in. He did and took a photograph from inside the cavity. The caption may have well read: 'The World Beyond a Pipe'. Part of the visual showed the dark interior of the cavity followed by the bright exterior, where lay the woods. The picture looked strange, but unique. This was his first ever photograph, and soon he was discovering the wonders of photography. But that day, Gopalakrishnan had made a statement.

The institute itself was experiencing and enjoying the novelty of being the country's first centre for serious cinema studies, and its professors were experimenting and trying to compile an imaginative teaching programme. And they came from various backgrounds and taught different things. Professor R.K. Ramachandran, brother of writer R.K. Narayan and cartoonist R.K. Laxman, handled editing. Guru Dutt's production manager, L.P. Shah, was teaching production, and he brought along with him his American training, having studied in California. There was an assistant professor of sound engineering, called S.B. Thakkar, whose lectures on the intriguing possibilities of sound recording were inspiring, though

Adoor first noticed the potential of sound from Ghatak, who he thought used it very 'theatrically'.

Adoor must have been really influenced by Thakkar, for the auteur takes great care about sound. He often spends weeks recording natural sounds, going back to his locations, after the principal shooting is over, trying to capture the gentle gurgle of a stream or the rustle of leaves or the chirping of a sparrow or the bleating of a lamb or the ring of a church bell.

I watched him during a sound-mixing session at Thiruvananthapuram's Chitranjali Studio, where he spent a long time trying to get the effects right. I remember this scene from *Naalu Pennungal*, where bridegroom Narayanan (played by Nandulal) is at his gluttonous best merrily tucking in food, and Gopalakrishnan was unbelievably patient ensuring that the noises the character made were perfect to the last note. I wonder how many poppadoms the sound-effects artist had to munch that morning before the director gave his by now trademark nod to the sound engineer N. Harikumar. The okay is a classic *kozhappam illa* ('no problem'/'it's okay').

Gopalakrishnan uses background music sparingly, sometimes never. In *Kodiyettam*, there is none. In the others, he is extremely judicious in its use, and highly sensitive to the way theatres handle the volume knob. At two festivals—in Chennai (December 2007) and Bengaluru (January 2008)—where *Naalu Pennungal* was shown, I saw him walk up to the projector room to ask the operator to tone down the volume. Much of the beauty of his visuals would be lost if sound and music were to be magnified into din and noise.

Another Pune professor whom Gopalakrishnan remembers with fondness is Satish Bahadur. He was an ardent fan of Ray, and used *Pather Panchali* extensively to explain how movies were made. Ray's debut feature was his Bible. He made a transcript of the film's script and circulated it among his students. And he showed the movie in different ways—with sound, without sound and sometimes only with sound and no images. This way, compositions, camera movements and the marvels of sound appeared clear, each in their own perspective or collectively to form the whole.

Years later, when Gopalakrishnan was a full-fledged director, he screened his *Kathapurushan* at the institute. Bahadur, who was still teaching there, was so impressed by it that he declared, then and there, that he would henceforth teach this film.

Did Bahadur, who loved Ray's work, see the master's influence on Gopalakrishnan's creations? I am not sure, but some critics place Gopalakrishnan in the Ray school of movie-making. There may have been two reasons for this. First, the younger director liked Ray's cinema, immensely so. Second, Ray used to say that Gopalakrishnan was his most favourite Indian director.

Adoor disagrees with the critics: 'Had my work resembled Ray's, he would have had nothing but disdain for me.' Gopalakrishnan is fiercely original, and he works very hard at being different, at creating something that is unique and novel. And I think he dislikes comparisons, more so if it has something to do with him.

Once when he was flying to Europe, a stewardess got around to talking to him and remarked in all her earnestness that he looked liked Albert Einstein. Gopalakrishnan was certainly not pleased and had retorted, 'That is not a compliment.' I wonder what the poor stewardess felt, but he can be brutally frank.

However, Gopalakrishnan admired Ray all right, an admiration that began at Gandhigram soon after the screening of *Pather Panchali*. Adoor writes in *Cinema Anubhavam*: 'I would liken Ray to a towering lighthouse. He, who stood over six feet tall, was an example and a guide to me and others in the cinema fraternity. He was a constant source of creative energy and inspiration.

Adoor further penned in the journal that 'If Indian cinema

can be divided into "Before Ray" and "After Ray", the central point of reference would be the *Apu* trilogy of *Pather Panchali*, *Aparajito* and *Apur Sansar*. Ray's films, which have uncommon beauty and internal integrity, shine like stars in the firmament of world cinema. They have a spirit of humanity running through them from the beginning to the end; display a great understanding of human nature; have humour and use simplicity to portray complex ideas. These qualities set Ray's work apart from other movies.'

And, Ray, in turn, was fond of Gopalakrishan's films. Ray always had a keen eye for young talent, fresh talent. After watching each of Gopalakrishnan's movies—from *Kodiyettam* to *Mathilukal* (based on Vaikom Muhammad Basheer's short story)—he would invite the young auteur to his place to give his opinion. 'I have only heard words of praise from him on each of my films, and never a word of adverse criticism,' Adoor is understandably proud.

Ray's response to *Mathilukal*—which was part of the 1990 International Film Festival of India at Kolkata—is something that Gopalakrishnan will cherish all his life. Ray was ill at that time with a bad heart, and his doctors had strictly forbidden him to climb stairs. And at the city's Gorky Sadan, where *Mathilukal* was to be shown, there was no lift, and an anxious Gopalakrishnan stood at the head of the stairs, wondering whether Ray would defy medical advice to watch the Malayalam entry. Mere minutes before the movie began, Ray got out of his car and slowly made his way up. This must have been a great moment for Gopalakrishnan.

After the screening, Ray clasped Gopalakrishnan's hands and said loudly, 'Marvellous Adoor.' Later, when some journalists asked Ray who his favourite Indian director was, he did not even pause for a second before he said in his famous baritone voice, 'Adoor, only Adoor.'

Derek Malcolm, a highly regarded British cinema critic, agrees with this. Talking to me on a warm sun-soaked day on the island of Lido during the 2007 Venice International Film Festival, he said, 'Adoor is one of the very best directors in India, has been for the past thirty years, somebody who does exactly what he wants to do. He never compromises. Quite like Ray, I would think. Adoor certainly has Ray's discipline. Adoor really thinks very hard about his films, thinks very hard about every shot, just like Ray. I think Adoor's technique is different from Ray's. Naturally so, because Ray's craft, picked up from Hollywood cinema, is very American. Gopalakrishnan's is not. But still he has the same rigour that Ray had,' Malcolm avers.

However, Gopalakrishnan's stories are more complex than Ray's. Ray was a romantic. Gopalakrishnan is not, and his stories are psychologically more probing than Ray's, psychologically deeper than Ray's.

Actor Murali, who was on the cast of *Mathilukal*, *Nizhalkkuthu* and *Naalu Pennungal*, says that his director is next only to Ray, a worthy successor to the master from Bengal. In some ways, Gopalakrishnan is greater than Ray. 'In India, very few directors have tried to break the realistic form. I have not seen even Ray do that. He, like many others, told stories. Period. Gopalakrishnan goes beyond that. He breaks the realistic form,' Murali contends.

What is more, Gopalakrishnan changes his style of narration with every work, and that makes his cinema extremely refreshing. We can hope to see the unexpected. We can be sure that there is a surprise waiting for us every time he gets behind the camera.

Till the 1970s, a celluloid work was as good as the story it said. But modern writers and poets changed this perception. Form and style took a precedence over content, and Gopalakrishnan was one of the first to make this switch in cinema.

And his cinema is an intimate portrayal of the life we see around us. The life as he knows best, the life in his native

Kerala. Like Ray, who never stepped outside Bengal to make films, Gopalakrishnan too stayed within the borders of the land he knew well or, at best, strayed a little outside, writing his own stories or occasionally borrowing from Basheer or Paul Zacharia (*Vidheyan*) or Thakazhi Sivasankara Pillai (*Naalu Pennungal* and *Oru Pennum Randaanum*/A Climate for Crime).

Ed Halter wrote in a 2003 edition of *Village Voice*, a weekly newspaper published in the USA: 'Like Satyajit Ray did with Bengal, Adoor Gopalakrishnan draws upon the history and aesthetics of his native region, Kerala. But where Ray's films glow with a bittersweet, redemptive humanism, Gopalakrishnan's recent features (*Vidheyan, Kathapurushan* and *Nizhalkkuthu*) analyze the darker aspects of society and existence with a forthrightness that affords few comforts. He sets social-realist tales within the detached, almost clinical structures of fairy tale and myth, confronting both negative and positive aspects of the human organism. Gopalakrishnan's worldview could be compared to the Marxist concept of dialectical struggle (minus utopian finale) or Hindu cosmology's inexorable yoking of creation to destruction.'

Gopalakrishnan's respect for Ghatak was as high as it was for Ray. Actually, at the institute, Ghatak's students became his greatest fans, particularly Mani Kaul and Kumar Shahani, who went about like Jesus Christ's apostles spreading the message of Ghatak! And there was a lot to say.

By the time Ghatak joined the institute, his most significant works had been made, and they included *Nagarik*, *Ajantrik* (Pathetic Fallacy, 1958), *Meghe Dhaka Tara* (*The Cloud-Capped Star*, 1960), *Komal Gandhar* (A Soft Note on a Sharp Scale, 1961) and *Subarnarekha* (The Golden Thread, 1962).

Gopalakrishnan, on the other hand, was too shy to get close to his teacher. While Gopalakrishnan's friends spent a lot of time with Ghatak in the institute's guesthouse where he stayed, Gopalakrishnan never did that. 'I could never walk up to somebody and start a conversation. Even today, I cannot do it.

I am basically an introvert,' he says. 'I do not even talk much. I am a listener.'

The only exception appears to be his days on the stage, and it is incredible that he could have acted in so many plays. But in cinema he made a complete switch, going behind the camera rather than facing it. He perhaps chose what he was most comfortable with.

At Pune, he spent much of his free time in the library, with the books he loved, companions he had grown so accustomed to from his childhood. After spending the first year at the institute reading plays and about playwrights, he made a neat shift in his second year, when he began studying cinema, serious books on it—theory and the aesthetics of it.

Pune was the intellectual capital of Maharashtra, and one could find there a great collection of books, cheap editions and second-hand ones. Such voracious reading obviously helped him to develop into an original thinker.

A look at his first movie, a twenty-minute fiction, he made as a student just before his course ended at Pune in 1965, is instructive. Called *A Great Day*, it was a comedy, a takeoff on himself. His protagonist is a lazy man, who loves to sleep late into the day. When the milkman would place the bottle outside the door, the hero had a rope attached to the door to open it.

When he falls in love with a woman, she wants him to meet her father. She asks her lover to tidy up his room before her father comes by. The man just cannot tidy up the mess, and the father arrives, says hello to him, gives him a look and goes away. The young man is sure that the whole thing must have been a disaster, when his girlfriend comes running in to tell him that her father liked him! And do you know why, she asks him. Because he loved your teeth. The father was a dentist!

Gopalakrishnan chose a man with a faultless set of gleaming white teeth to play the role. And to me, there is so much of Chaplin in this work, the humour, the biographical streak, the comic picturization all seem to remind me of the great tramp.

However, the attempt goes beyond the Chaplinesque, and that is what his work is all about. A dash of novelty and a streak of originality.

Wit—restrained and subdued—and often conveyed through sheer images, has been an integral part of Gopalakrishnan's cinema. Take, for instance, *Naalu Pennungal*, where Narayanan's gorging has been attracting laughs the world over, from Chennai to Thiruvananthapuram to Bengaluru to Toronto to Nantes and Warsaw. Humour can be universal, provided it is done with finesse.

Forty-five years after Gopalakrishnan graduated in 1965, I wonder whether he would have ever become a movie-maker, and a great one at that, had he not entered the portals of the Pune Film Institute. Probably not. What does Adoor himself have to say about this? 'Never'. In a single word, he conveys the institute's phenomenal role in getting him interested in and appreciative of cinema, the first step towards becoming a renowned auteur.

8

Missionary of
Meaningful Movies

Gopalakrishnan's growing passion for cinema led to a
burning desire to herald a film society movement in
Kerala. At Pune, he assembled a small group of individuals and
called it Chitralekha Film Unit. These individuals came from
different faculties of the institute, like cinematography, sound,
editing, screenplay writing and direction. They planned to
work together after their graduation. They had three aims:
start a film society movement, publish serious literature on
cinema, and produce, distribute and exhibit meaningful movies.

The fifth All-India Writers' Conference at Alwaye, Kerala, in
January 1966 provided a wonderful opportunity for
Gopalakrishnan and his team to get this movement off the
ground. They organized screenings of fifteen world classics—
to coincide with the conference—in the state's nine districts as
well as the bordering Nagercoil in Tamil Nadu. Vans carrying
prints criss-crossed the region pushing and promoting a novel
cinema culture, and arousing public interest in different genres.

Works such as *Cranes are Flying* (Mikhail Kalatozov, USSR), *Ballad of a Soldier* (Grigori Chukhrai, USSR), *Knife in the Water* (Roman Polanski, Poland), *Night Train* (Jerzy Kawalerowicz, Poland), *La Verite* (George Clouzot, France), *Skylark* (Laszlo Ranody, Hungary), *Macario* (Roberts Gavaldon, Mexico), *Devi* (Satyajit Ray, India) and *Meghe Dhaka Tara* (Ritwik Ghatak, India) were screened.

Gopalakrishnan knew some writers and literary stalwarts of the time, such as M. Govindan, C.N. Sreekantan Nair and M.K.K. Nayar (a great connoisseur of arts and letters). The young man's passion and zeal for the cause of good cinema must have led Govindan to ask Gopalakrishnan if he would organize an international cinema event to add a new dimension to the Writers' Conference. Gopalakrishnan was only too keen, and the film festival proved to be a landmark event whose impact reverberated throughout the state and its neighbourhood.

Those were the days when cinema enjoyed little respect among intellectuals or universities. The festival helped place cinema alongside literature and other arts, and Gopalakrishnan hoped that the event would create awareness—at least in the towns the festival had been hosted—for a cinema that went beyond entertainment. It did and in many ways, this festival gave a fillip to the film society movement in Kerala. In about a decade after 1966, the state had about 110 societies (the largest number in any region, a record previously held by West Bengal) with men like G. Aravindan, another exceptional helmer, and P. Padmarajan, actively participating in them. Both made movies later.

Long before all this, the country's first film society—Amateur Cine Society—was established in Mumbai in 1937. Headed by Stanley Jepson, editor of the *Illustrated Weekly of India*, the organization wanted to make short movies. Five years later, some documentary makers formed the Bombay Film Society to familiarize themselves with trends in Western cinema.

But it was the Calcutta Film Society, formed in 1947 under the leadership of Ray, movie-maker Nemai Ghosh (director of *Chinnamool*/The Uprooted, and not Ray's still photographer Nemai Ghosh) and cinema critic/director Chidananda Das Gupta, that envisaged the role of a film society movement in a qualitatively different manner and in the sense in which we understand it today. The society bridged the gap between big-banner Indian cinema and Hollywood fare, dominating the then theatrical scene, by screening mostly European movies. The society's membership grew.

In Kerala, Gopalakrishnan and his Gandhigram classmate and close friend Kulathoor Bhaskaran Nair set up the Chitralekha Film Society in Thiruvananthapuram in July 1965. It laid the foundation for a film society movement in the state, and helped form cinema clubs in universities and colleges. The cinema festival that took place six months later firmed up the movement.

Adoor says: 'There were two important reasons why we started the society. One, I wanted to continue watching the best of international movies. Two, I wanted to introduce audiences to a different kind of cinema. And tell them, "Look, it is not the song-and-dance kind of cinema alone that is being produced." There are many other kinds of cinema being made elsewhere in the world.'

The society published thought-provoking literature on cinema. The first publication was planned and executed even when Gopalakrishnan was at Pune, and the articles spoke not about star lives or their love affairs or sexual escapades, but film technique, technological innovations, performances, direction, scripts and so on. The journal was the first of its kind in Malayalam and included writings by eminent personalities, such as Ray, Ghatak, Abbas, cinematographer Mankada Ravi Varma, actor Balraj Sahani, Das Gupta, veteran journalist B.K. Karanjia, writer Marie Seton and Professor Satish Bahadur. A photo feature on world classics and a glossary of technical terms added to its uniqueness.

As much as Ray's writings and cinematic work excited and motivated Gopalakrishnan, the Bengal master's role in the film society movement was no less a guiding force for the young student from Pune. Others also pushed Gopalakrishnan to spread the magic of the medium. Professor Bahadur himself had been a member of the Patna Film Society. Seton, who wrote a biography of Ray (*Satyajit Ray: Portrait of a Director*) in 1978, spoke about film appreciation at Pune, and listening to people like her invigorated Gopalakrishnan and strengthened his resolve.

Actually, the Chitralekha Film Society was a wing of the Chitralekha Film Cooperative, registered in 1965, soon after Gopalakrishnan passed out of Pune. It was established with the help of a large number of friends and well-wishers. Many contributed to this, the Kerala government too, with shared participation. 'So, we had a paid-up share capital, meagre though it was,' Adoor contends. This was the first time a cooperative of this kind had been set up in the country to produce, distribute and exhibit pictures. The film society was part of the exhibition and education process: to spread a healthy culture by screening a different kind of celluloid fare and publishing serious literature on it.

Meera Sahib, a long-time friend and chief assistant of Gopalakrishnan, tells me that 'the cooperative broke the vicious monopoly of Kerala's theatre owners who controlled finance, production, distribution and, of course, exhibition. One could hardly watch anything other than mostly Tamil and Malayalam blockbusters that were boringly repetitive, cliché ridden and formula driven.'

The cooperative sought to address these issues, and succeeded. Kerala became a notable centre for small, sensible and sensitive cinema. Jnanpith Award winner, M.T. Vasudevan Nair's *Nirmalyam* (The Offering, 1973), Aravindan's *Uttarayanam* (Throne of Capricorn, 1974), K.G. George's *Swapnadanam* (Journey through a Dream, 1975) and John Abraham's

Agraharathil Kazhuthai (A Donkey in a Brahmin Street, 1978) followed Gopalakrishnan's 1972 *Swayamvaram*, and together they pioneered the Indian New Wave* in Kerala.

On a wider, pan-Indian scale, the New Wave was initiated by Mrinal Sen (*Bhuvan Shome*/Mr Shome, 1969), Mani Kaul (*Uski Roti*/Daily Bread, 1969) and Basu Chatterjee (*Sara Akash*/The Whole Sky, 1969), all of whom used Hindi. They are considered to be the first in the country to produce this kind of alternative or parallel cinema, uniquely different from the formulaic rest.

In the next few years, many others made such cinema. Pattabhi Rama Reddy's *Samskara* (Ritual), based on Jnanpith Award winner U.R. Ananthamurthy's novel by the same name, was a path-breaking Kannada work of 1970. In Mumbai, Kumar Sahani's *Maya Darpan* (Magic Mirror, 1972), Awtar Krishna Kaul's *27 Down* (1973), M.S. Sathyu's *Garam Hawa* (Hot Wind, 1974) and Shyam Benegal's *Ankur* (The Seedling, 1974) were great efforts to pull cinema away from the rut it had got into.

Even earlier than the 1970s, there were attempts at off-beat cinema, though they were not fully accomplished: in Tamil, *Unnaippol Oruvan* (Someone Like You) by famous Tamil writer and Jnanpith Award winner, Jayakanthan; and in Malayalam, Ramu Kariat's and P. Bhaskaran's *Neela Kuyil* (Blue Cuckoo) and P.N. Menon's *Olavum Theeravum* (Waves and the Shore) were a few.

The Chitralekha Cooperative—which built a full-fledged studio, including a recording theatre, a processing laboratory and editing facilities—helped produce a different kind of cinema. Gopalakrishan's first two works, *Swayamvaram* and

---

*While the Indian New Wave was largely influenced by the French *La Nouvella Vague*, Ray's 1955 *Pather Panchali* was inspired by Italian Neo-Realism, more specifically Vittorio de Sica's *The Bicycle Thief*.

Kodiyettam, and several documentaries, Aravindan's debut work, *Uttarayanam*, and many other ground-breaking movies emerged from the studio or with the help of its equipment.

In those days, Gopalakrishnan and others wanted to make films at any cost. Having learnt the craft at Pune and craving for expression, they were extremely eager to translate all that they had studied into motion pictures, documenting life in its many manifestations.

He gave himself five years after his graduation from Pune to make his first movie, five years of struggle. 'And I struggled not for five, but seven years. I never waited for something to happen, but I kept working, not necessarily on a feature or a documentary, but on other things. I kept the film society going, visited universities and colleges and screened movies there and gave lectures on cinema to students,' he says.

In short, he became a missionary of meaningful cinema—cinema that was real, that spoke about real people and real issues and was set in real locales. It follows that Gopalakrishnan's first film, *Swayamvaram*, made in 1972, was his contribution to meaningful cinema.

Swayamvaram and the rest that followed were in some ways akin to the Dogma 95 cinema, a label given by Danish directors 23 years after Gopalakrishnan's first work opened—a fact that merely reiterates that Indians had to their credit innumerable firsts in a variety of fields.

Dogme 95 (*dogme* being the Danish word for dogma) is an avant-garde film-making movement started in 1995 by renowned Danish directors Lars von Trier and Thomas Vinterberg. Two other Danish helmers, Kristian Levring and Soren Kragh-Jacobsen, later came on board to form a group known as Dogme 95 Collective or Dogme Brethren. They signed a manifesto—whose first paragraphs mimic French auteur François Truffaut's 1954 essay, '*Une certaine tendance du cinéma Français*' in *Cahiers du Cinéma*—and took a Vow of Chastity. It was a simple pledge to take cinema back to its origins, and this meant no props, no artificial lighting, filming on actual locations and using handheld cameras. Von Trier's *Breaking the Waves* (1996) followed these rules, but not fully. Some more movies were made on these lines, but the movement appears to have petered out.

There were similarities between the Dogme films and Gopalakrishnan's work, though I would think that it is closest to Ray's and Ghatak's reality cinema, 'Indian reality' as Adoor likes to call it. More specifically, Bengal's reality. Ray's pictures mirror the period and place in great detail, as do Gopalakrishnan's, which can be invaluable social documents. The flavour of the times and the ways of the people can be seen in his works. We learn so much about customs and costumes as we do about mannerisms and moods.

Adoor says each of his movies faithfully records the history of a particular period, the time in which it is set. Hence, he makes sure of the authenticity of the facts and materials used. For *Mathilukal*, he got hold of a jail administration manual of the 1920s, and studied it to recreate the right ambience and details in the prison scenes.

Vidheyan, for example, tells us about migrant Christian settlers on the Kerala–Karnataka border and the dying powers of the once ruling class, Patelars. The film is authentic to the point of even using furniture from that time. Remember the chair without an arm that Bhaskara Patelar (enacted by Mammootty) uses. Gopalakrishnan had a trying time finding it. So also the bed on which Tanvi Azmi's Saroja is murdered.

Again, *Kathapurushan* is highly representative of the period; it presents a graphic view of the changing political scenario in which Gandhian values and idealism are gradually crushed by extreme forms of political movements, such as the peasant-driven Naxalism, and autocratic state power, culminating in the promulgation of the Emergency in June 1975 under the prime ministership of Indira Gandhi.

This is the cinema that Gopalakrishnan produced, honest

and engaging. This is the kind of cinema he loved, and this is the kind of cinema he pushed and promoted, often lugging movie reels on his scooter for the next show. And the next.

Sadly, the Chitralekha Film Society faded into oblivion in the 1980s. So did the Chitralekha Film Cooperative, and the most important cause of this was Gopalakrishnan's disassociation from both. His differences primarily with Nair led to Gopalakrishnan's exit, and like many other institutions in India which weaken and wind up after that one man bids adieu, Chitralekha too floundered after its very spirit and soul left.

9

Beginnings and Beyond

Gopalakrishnan was beginning to get restless. He had mastered the grammar and practice of cinema, feasted on masterpieces and minor pieces, and spread the goodness around through a flourishing film society movement. He even started a cooperative dedicated to making good cinema. But there was no work to get his hands on, to chew on, so to say. Not really. The late 1960s were hard times, when even assignments for shorts or documentaries came in trickles, if at all.

It was on one such day that a message arrived from a favourite professor of his, Satish Bahadur. The 1967 Montreal Expo had a competition section on experimental cinema where fifty-second shorts were to be screened. The theme was *Man and the World*. Send your entries, the Expo said. Yes, send yours, Bahadur pushed his young student. Gopalakrishnan felt charged.

He had just helped his friend K.T. John finish a documentary on Maharaja Swathi Thirunal for the Films Division of India. The shoot over, there was some raw stock left, and with John's camera, Gopalakrishnan captured what he had conceptualized.

He got hold of an old worker in the press, his theatre pal Karamana, a beautiful young woman and a cute child to play in his movie that narrated their individual stories about desires, old age and death. He took it to Ramnord Laboratory in Mumbai (then Bombay), edited it, titled it *The Myth* and sent the reel to Montreal. Hundreds of such reels arrived at the Canadian Quebec City. Literally hundreds.

But Gopalakrishnan's stood out, and was adjudged to be among the best twenty, and became part of the Canadian Cinematheque's valuable collection. It was his first film after graduation, and, quite understandably, he was proud and happy.

'What happened after that?' I asked him imagining fame and offers to have flooded in.

'Nothing spectacular,' he said in his classic low-key manner.

He managed to find work, though, and made some documentaries. He had to. To satisfy his passion and his need. 'I was itching to make movies. It could be in any format, any subject, any length. It could be a documentary, an information film or even a publicity picture. I did not mind. But no publicity movies were being made those days in Kerala. A few government and quasi-government organizations were commissioning information films,' Adoor says.

He got a contract from the Kerala State Electricity Board to make a movie on the famous Idukki Hydroelectric Project. The board wanted him to document the entire construction of a huge arch dam (one of the highest in Asia) between two mountains in Kerala's Idukki district. Built with Canadian aid, work began in April 1969, and the dam, the reservoir and the underground powerhouse were commissioned by Prime Minister Indira Gandhi in February 1976, bang in the middle of the draconian Emergency. Most politicians of the opposition were in jail, and a feeling of suspicion, conspiracy, fear and even horror prevailed in the entire country, and it is in such dreadful times that Idukki rose out of the Periyar River.

The project, one of the most prestigious in India, was to have been completed in four years, but was delayed by three years. Was it good for Gopalakrishnan? Not really. He and his team got a small amount of money, and they had to cover each stage of execution. They had no money to hire a van, and so they would take a bus from Thiruvananthapuram to Idukki, a good six hours away, lugging an old Arriflex camera and a couple of lights that needed no stands. They were a three-member team with Gopalakrishnan handling the camera, an assistant and a light boy.

It was an hour long documentary, and it turned out to be quite interesting, showing just about every phase of the project. One could see the dam growing on the screen, but sadly the work is all but lost. Processed at Chennai's AVM laboratory, the black-and-white negative has disappeared. No one knows where the print is. Does one exist at all?

Gopalakrishnan made more documentaries. He remembers doing one on State Lottery, another on handicrafts (*And Man Created*, 1968) and a few on family planning. These helped him experiment with the camera, an invaluable extension of the theory classes on cinematography at Pune.

For twenty years between the late 1960s and the late 1980s, he did four documentaries in collaboration with painter Velu Viswanadhan. Hailing from Kollam in Kerala, he now lives part of the year in the Cholamandal Artists' Village—which he helped found in the mid-1960s—on the Bay of Bengal, just outside Chennai. The rest of the year, he lives in Paris, and is often known as Paris Viswanadhan.

The four documentaries that Gopalakrishnan did for him are etched in memory. One was on *Kalam* and *Padmam* (titled *Form and Colour*). *Kalam* is the art of creating figures, generally of the goddess Kali, with various indigenous coloured powders, while *Padmam* are highly intricate and sophisticated designs made within rectangles and circles, filled in with coloured powders. *Padmam* form part of *Tantrik* rites, and has influenced many modern Indian artists. Gopalakrishnan shot *Form and Colour* in 16 mm, and his association with the painter that began in 1965 during the All India Writers' Conference led to this collaboration.

After this, Viswanadhan came up with the idea of collecting sand from different points on the Indian coast. 'He was a compulsive traveller,' remarks Adoor. 'We—my art director Sivan [for seven of Gopalakrishnan's movies from *Kodiyettam* to *Kathapurushan*], and poets Kadammanitta Ramakrishnan [noted Left-wing bard who took Malayalam poetry out of the ivory tower and to the masses] and Pazhavila N. Ramesan [another non-conformist writer]—began our journey from the Kerala coast, drove up to West Bengal through the southern tip of India, Kanyakumari, cut across the breadth of the country to the sea shores of Gujarat in Western India and came down to Kerala again collecting sand at every place. The sand colour varied dramatically from region to region. Viswanadhan used the sand to create pictures, and I filmed him at work and life on the shores.' This documentary, *Sand*, shot on Super 8, was a long see at seven hours.

The journey also helped Gopalakrishnan brush up his rusty Hindi, and with every passing day, he found his language skills improving. The rest of the team could barely manage to communicate with local residents, and Gopalakrishnan soon became a captain of sorts of the team, even taking turns with Sivan to be at the wheel.

The painter then fell in love with the Ganga, the holiest of Indian rivers, and Gopalakrishnan went along with him capturing the essence of the river. It is part of Indian folklore, mythology and, indeed, of life itself on whose banks grew a great culture.

The almost 2500-kilometre-long Ganga originates at the Gangotri glacier on the Himalayan range of mountains that stretches across Myanmar, India, Tibet, Bhutan, Nepal, Pakistan and Afghanistan, and feeds two major river systems—the

Indus and the Ganga–Brahmaputra—before flowing into the Bay of Bengal. The river and its tributaries drain a large— about a million square kilometres—and fertile basin that supports one of the world's most densely populated regions.

The Ganga has been revered and worshipped by the Hindus for centuries. Nehru wrote in his book, *Discovery of India*: 'The Ganges (Ganga), above all, is the river of India, which has held India's heart captive and drawn uncounted millions to her banks since the dawn of history. The story of the Ganges, from her source to the sea, from old times to new, is the story of India's civilization and culture, of the rise and fall of empires, of great and proud cities, of adventures of man . . .'

Viswanadhan and Gopalakrishnan began their own adventure at Sagar Island in Bengal, where the Ganga breaks into hundreds of streams and empties into the sea. From there they motored and trekked along the river to its origin at Gomukh, eighteen kilometres uphill from Gangotri.

The Gangotri glacier stretches up to Gomukh and the trudge was highly treacherous with boulders tumbling down the mountain slope. There were times when the director and his friend had to dart across the pathway or ahead to avoid being hit, nay smashed. The path itself was narrow, flanked by the high Himalayan hills and steep drops into valleys, and Adoor considers this trip as the most perilous in his life yet. He says the Mahabharata rightly describes this journey as *mahaprasthana*, which literally means 'never-to-return departure'. Happily, the two men came back home. Not, though, before an extremely thrilling—and, yes, fulfilling— mission.

At every step, Gopalakrishnan recorded the sights and sounds that somehow seemed to blend with the mighty river, sometimes gently gurgling like a newborn and at other times furiously gushing down, threatening to carry away anything that came in its way. Along the banks, the songs that nomadic mendicants sang and the musical notes from the instruments they played added to the richness of the region—and to the celluloid work. There was one who played the flute with an almost masterly touch, and he became one of the high points of the documentary.

Between Gangotri and Gomukh, there was no hotel and the two rested at night in an ashram, which offered free food and blankets. The head of the hermitage, a sage, served food to his guests. Probably, he himself had cooked it, for his arms bore telltale signs of burns. That night, Gopalakrishnan could hardly sleep. He was crammed into a room with many others. Lying between a sheet and a coarse blanket, he tossed and turned, the snores from the other boarders ruining his sleep. The roar of the river outside sounded eerie, adding to his restlessness. And sometime before dawn, he had a dream. The river was rising dangerously, and the water, gushing out, was swallowing just about everything. The ashram, the surroundings and the valley itself were disappearing under the vast sheet of water. The first rays of sunlight shook him out of this terrifying ordeal.

A documentary made under such trying conditions won rave reviews. Titled *Ganga*, it walked away with the Grand Prize at Paris' Cinema du Reel Festival, and became a forerunner of many movies on the river.

With Gopalakrishnan handling the camera, he had one great advantage. He was always ready to freeze on frame rare sights of nature and life. And he was intuitive. He knew when something was coming, and he kept his camera ready and running.

Once on a huge bed of sand, so large that it looked like a desert, near Allahabad—the city where the three rivers, the Ganga, the Yamuna and the mythical Saraswati, form a confluence called Sangam—he saw a storm gather and gain strength. And when the swirling sand hit, he caught it on film. 'I stood in the raging sandstorm, camera in hand, photographing the sequence. It turned out to be awesomely beautiful,' Adoor says remembering the day.

At Kakdwip, in Bengal, nature offered many more such

wonders. Lightning played hide and seek among dark, frightening clouds, and when the rain stopped, the rays of the sun created fascinating patterns in the sky. 'I have never seen something so ethereal,' Adoor was clearly enchanted. There was another occasion in the same state when the receding waters of the river exposed a bewildering variety of fish and other forms of life.

Ganga ran two hours and thirty minutes, and became a favourite with audiences. This was the second of a five-part series that Viswanadhan had planned on the five elements of nature. Gopalakrishnan did three, sand (earth), water and fire, the last though not fully.

For the documentary on fire, they criss-crossed the country, and Gopalakrishnan saw this magnificent phenomenon at a place called Jwalamukhi at the foothills of the Himalayas: a raging natural fire and a temple and a township built around it, a goddess breathing flames, and the rocks around aflame. Nature at its fearsome glory that devotees flocked to see.

Though the ideas for the documentaries came from Viswanadhan, these were developed into movies by Gopalakrishnan. He had the perfect freedom to do so. An absolute necessity for an artist, much more so for Gopalakrishnan.

In some ways, Viswanadhan is like Gopalakrishnan. The painter, according to one website biography of his, 'is of the opinion that when put in a protected environment, the creative intensity will not unleash itself. One should break free from the nestled environs to channel the creative energy properly. Once it is attained, the way things would project becomes different, and there will be more insight into unfolding things . . .'

Later, Gopalakrishnan got choosy about his subjects. He said to himself that he would make documentaries only on the performing arts. And he did, turning out some of the most amazing ones I have ever seen on Kathakali and Mohiniattam among others.

10

Documenting the Dramatic

As his camera rolled, panned and tilted, Gopalakrishnan embraced some ideas, forsook some others. He has made about thirty shorts and documentaries on various subjects, but since the past three decades he has been consciously training his camera on Kerala's performing arts, studying and savouring them to document their magnificent past, their exciting present and their hopefully bright future.

'In the beginning, I made documentaries on any subject,' Adoor says and there were reasons for this. 'I had to survive, and the institution I set up had to. Chitralekha needed work, because there were many who depended on it to live.'

But I suppose a time came towards the close of the 1970s when he found that his association with Chitralekha was beginning to weigh on him like an albatross. Much like Samuel Taylor Coleridge's poem, *The Rime of the Ancient Mariner* (1798), where an albatross following a ship is first seen as a good omen, but later as evil and is shot, Chitralekha began impeding Gopalakrishnan's professional progress. His dream turned into disillusionment, and what gave him so much joy led to sorrow later.

His impending exit from Chitralekha signalled his new resolve to concentrate on the performing arts. 'I enjoyed doing these documentaries because I loved learning about the arts. I did my own research, and I discovered so much about our past in the process,' Adoor tells me.

For instance, a Sanskrit theatre like Koodiyattam is the oldest living theatre in the world. How many people know that? It is some 2000 years old. One of Kerala's tenth-century rulers, Kulasekhara Varman who developed Koodiyattam into its present form wrote two plays, *Subhadradhananjayam* and *Thapathi Swayamvaram*. It also finds mention in the 1500-year-old Tamil classic, Ilangovan's *Silappadikaram*—the story of Kovalan, his wife, Kannagi and his lover, Madhavi.

In 2001, Koodiyattam won a rare honour when the United Nations Educational, Scientific and Cultural Organization (UNESCO) declared it a masterpiece of human heritage to be protected and preserved. There were thirty-one other art forms from all over the world that year vying for this privilege, and they included Japan's Nogaku theatre, China's Kunqu opera and Spain's Elche play, but it was Koodiyattam that stole the show.

And Gopalakrishnan was the man who in his genteel manner drew the attention of the UNESCO jury in Paris to Koodiyattam. The members saw just fifteen minutes of a three-hour documentary on Koodiyattam by him, and were floored. This was the first time ever that UNESCO was conferring a heritage status on an oral tradition. Koodiyattam certainly deserved it, but had it not been for Gopalakrishnan's brilliant documentary, scripted and assisted by Sudha Gopalakrishnan (a scholar on Koodiyattam), the Paris jury might have never understood the enormous significance of this theatre, and the need for it to live and flourish.

But to make that documentary, the man had to fight, first of all to carry his camera inside a *koothambalam*. Literallly, it means temple for theatre—a marvellous structure, perfect in acoustics and exclusively used for staging Koodiyattam—and is part of some grand Hindu temples in Kerala. Koothambalam is as sacred as the sanctum sanctorum of the main temple. And what is more, only men and women of the Chakyar community can perform Koodiyattam inside a koothambalam. Others are not usually allowed there.

But Gopalakrishnan was determined to cross these hurdles, and how he made the documentary reads like a sensational movie plot.

Once he had made up his mind, he began his search for the most impressive koothambalam. His hunt took him beyond Kottayam, and he saw koothambalams in Thirussur, Haripad, Irinjalakuda, and many other places. He was not quite impressed by these, till his journey took him to Kidangoor, a beautiful village between Kottayam and Pala divided by the Meenachil River. On the southern side lies the 1500-year-old Subramanya Swamy Temple in which Gopalakrishnan saw the finest of koothambalams. It was love at first sight in a very classic sort of way, and he decided that his documentary on Koodiyattam would be set there.

The temple is owned by a few Brahmin families, whose permission he sought and even received. However, when he was all set to begin his shoot, he got telephone calls from strangers who warned him against filming inside the koothambalam. A day before the camera was to roll, an ultimatum came: do not shoot there or face the consequences. Gopalakrishnan was prepared to do just that.

The Chakyars who had assembled there to perform were visibly nervous, and they advised their director to pack and leave, not to quarrel with the protestors, rowdies that they were. But Gopalakrishnan was not one to run away, and at almost midnight the day before work was to begin, he met the district collector, 'a nice young man', who asked the police to round up the potential trouble-makers.

A few hours later, the shoot began, but not before the

cameramen were coaxed out of their hotel room, where they had closeted themselves hoping that their director would have packed up. The work progressed, and the documentary created history. The director of UNESCO flew to Thiruvananthapuram to watch the documentary, three hours in all, and so impressed was she by it that she at once made plans for the UNESCO board and jury to see it.

Originally, the documentary was ten hours long, but was later edited down to three. Of these, the UNESCO jury saw barely fifteen minutes and decided to honour one of the greatest oral traditions the world has ever known.

By the time Gopalakrishnan shot the documentary, he had a fair idea of this theatre, having learnt about it by watching innumerable performances. Appukuttan Nair, founder of Margi (a centre for advanced training in Koodiyattam and Kathakali), renowned scholar of Koodiyattam and chief engineer in Kerala's Public Health and Engineering Department, was fond of him and began taking him to the shows, where he learnt the nuances of this art form and began appreciating them.

Adoor reminisces, 'I was not very close to Koodiyattam at that time. I had hardly seen any of it, and I did not care much, because it was too difficult to access this form. Once Nair asked me to go along with him to watch a concert. So I went with him.' Gopalakrishnan must have been greatly attracted to it, for he began to accompany him every Friday to watch this theatre. Gopalakrishnan gradually realized that Kathakali, an art form he had grown up with, was simpler than Koodiyattam, and more popular.

Sitting on Nair's right at every Friday show, a special place that only the privileged were entitled to, Gopalakrishnan was initiated into Koodiyattam. It took a few years, but it happened, and his fledgling curiosity for it grew into a lifelong passion.

Koodiyattam has a set of rigid conventions: for instance, no performance can take place unless there is at least one scholar of this art seated in the front row. Yet Gopalakrishnan's documentary was screened to a jury that knew very little about this theatre. Maybe, nothing at all. There was none there initiated into it. No scholar of the art. However, it is in this scenario that Koodiyattam emerged from Kerala's languorous backwaters to be fêted and feasted upon in the global arena.

I really wonder how in the first place Gopalakrishnan made a mere three-hour documentary on a theatre that is unimaginably long: it takes fifteen to forty-five days for just a single act to be staged, and an epic like the Ramayana may well take a year to unfold. The UNESCO jury saw a mere fifteen minutes: maybe, they saw the most significant quarter hour. Or, was the documentary so well and tightly shot that every frame had the power to enslave a viewer?

Whatever it may have been, Gopalakrishnan's role in reviving Koodiyattam will be written in the annals of Indian art history.

He has two guiding principles before doing a documentary. He would take up a project only when he is fascinated by it, and the research he does himself goes a long way in helping him understand the subject in its most minute detail. And when the film emerges out of the cans, it wows us.

Like his latest, *Mohiniattam: Dance of the Enchantress*. Adoor says that he has been waiting to document this form for almost twenty-five years. This is more of a non-fiction feature rather than strictly a documentary. 'The traditional concept of a documentary has already undergone changes,' Adoor explains. It is more than just a record of events. It has gone beyond that. And his latest documentary does precisely that.

Although it does not work on the element of fiction, it has the appearance of one. But Adoor contends that he was merely trying to heighten 'a certain reality'. What is this reality: a girl, who is learning Mohiniattam from a guru. She is a dreamer, in love, waiting for him, longing for him. Gopalakrishnan interweaves this romance with the seductive appeal of the dance, and he choreographs it with such finesse that the images and music blend into rhythmic harmony. So perfect is the composition of each frame, so ethereally lit, that it begins to glow with supreme joy.

The girl's fantasy is portrayed with pain and pleasure: her wait, her union, her motherhood and finally her separation from the man she adored. At the end, we see her putting the baby to sleep with the lullaby, *Omanathinkal Kidavo* . . .

In contrast, we see her teacher—a single parent nurturing her little daughter and facing life's hurdles and handicaps. These seem pitted against her student's flight of imagination. The teacher is a great performer, and her student a passionate learner.

As Adoor tells us these two stories, he also explains how Lord Vishnu took the form of a beautiful damsel to entice the demons, the real enemies of the gods, and take away the nectar from them. As 'she' turns each demon into a state of stupor, Lord Shiva, the great cosmic dancer, finds himself attracted to Mohini. So goes the story, and the movie.

'And if you analyse the film, you will also see that there are visual pauses in it. These pauses relate to the life lived in Kerala. I am constantly trying to relate Mohiniattam to the real people who gave life to it, whose culture has flowered in this art form,' Adoor tells me how his *Enchantress* enthralls audiences.

Earlier in 2005, he made a documentary on Kalamandalam Ramankutty Nair (the documentary was of the same name), who was past eighty then. The oldest performing artist in Kathakali, he is not very well now. Funded and produced by the Sangeet Natak Akademi, this work is biographical and the story is told in the first person singular. Gopalakrishnan did not want to use a commentary. Rather, he let Ramankutty talk, and this gives the documentary a feel of authenticity.

Ramankutty's life is one of total dedication to Kathakali. Fascinated by this form of theatre, he left school and trained under the legend, Pattikkanthodi Ravunni Menon. Fighting poverty and other hardships, Ramankutty went on to become a great artist, a teacher in Kerala Kalamandalam at Shornur and eventually its principal, educating some who became accomplished artists of this theatre form.

The documentary is a tribute to him, and we see the man and his aesthetics unravel with every reel. Wonderfully conceptualized, the work respects Ramankutty's space, though the shoot itself was not free of hassles.

Gopalakrishnan, who knew him, added to the script, drawn from a biography of his. The director wrote Ramankutty's dialogues, but Ramankutty was not very comfortable being directed, because he had always been a teacher and was never used to being told what to do. For years, he had been the principal of Kalamandalam, and one is told that he used to terrorize his students. A time came when the two giants, one of cinema and the other of theatre clashed.

Nonetheless, when Ramankutty saw the documentary, he was so overwhelmed that he quipped, 'Now I am ready to die.' Admittedly, the work was a splendid effort by one who grew up watching Kathakali. And whose family had been ardent patrons of this art for generations. The documentary effortlessly juxtaposes the past with the present, and in a series of sequences, Gopalakrishnan allows Ramankutty to ramble on about his yesterdays. There are times when the two periods mix and mingle to form a whole.

The movie underlines Ramankutty's childlike innocence and immense talent. Renowned for his portrayal of valiant kings, Ramankutty playing Keechaka in *Keechaka Vadham*, a part of the Mahabharata, was a treat to behold.

Kathakali and Mohiniattam are but two of Kerala's several classical and folk arts. Indeed, there are hundreds of them, and most of them, especially the folk forms, are dying. But Gopalakrishnan has not filmed any of these, concentrating on the classical alone. He has made three documentaries on Kathakali: *Guru Chenganoor* (1974), *Kalamandalam Gopi* (1999) and *Kalamandalam Ramankutty Nair* (2005).

Kalamandalam Gopi grew up in poverty, but two benevolent

Namboodiri families initiated him into Kathakali. Kalamandalam shaped his craft to perfection. We catch rare glimpses from his life and art as he transforms himself into different forms.

The Films Division wanted Gopalakrishnan to do a twenty-minute documentary on Gopi. But that would have been ridiculous: 'You cannot do justice to the artiste, a lead performer at that, and the art in such a short length. I had to have at least six performances, and finally I did have my way. I got forty-seven minutes, though I managed with the original budget.'

Shooting was elaborate with about hundred people on the set and two cameras that captured every twitch on Gopi's face, every nuance of his incredible innocence. And, the story, narrated by the man himself, tells us of his trials and tribulations. One such was the slipped disc he suffered from, and doctors pronounced he would never dance again. But he rose to prove them wrong, and said that he would like to die performing.

Apart from these, Adoor filmed, in 1982, *Krishnanattam*, which is considered a forerunner to Kathakali. Krishnanattam is one of his favourites. Essentially a temple art, which originated in and is confined to the Guruvayur Sri Krishna Temple, Krishnanattam narrates the story of Krishna in a series of eight plays: *Avataram, Kaliyamardanam, Rasakrida, Kamsavadham, Swayamvaram, Banayuddham, Vividavadham* and *Swargarohanam*. Krishnanattam has more dance in it, and liberally uses masks, unlike in Kathakali, where an elaborately painted face resembles a mask. In Krishnanattam, the masks represent characters. Mudras or the hand gestures are used minimally, and they are simple. These are the essential differences between the two classical forms.

Gopalakrishnan's documentaries may well be called invaluable treatises on Kerala's classical art forms, particularly Kathakali. Long, long ago, he fell in love with this art as he sat on his mother's lap, completely mesmerized by the painted faces with large headgears that swayed in front of him. That evening, the lady could have never imagined that her tiny son would some day document Kathakali in all its dramatic grandeur.

11

The Sound of Silence

Lately, I have been noticing a trend which disturbs me. In cinemas, the moment there is silence on the screen, people get restive. Even babies begin bawling, completely ruining the serenity of silence that some directors have begun to use. Audiences are not comfortable with visuals without voice. They want constant flow of decibels usually in the form of music. The higher the decibel, the better. The more continuous the background score, the greater the comfort. Or, so it seems.

Admittedly, in the structure of cinema, music is the most noticeable feature of sound, which, if used with care, becomes a 'creative presence'. Otherwise, it jars. Sadly, very little attention is paid to background score in Indian cinema: many use it to hide directorial defects, incompetent acting and other shortcomings.

Sometimes, the background music is so loud that dialogues seem unclear. At other times, music is so constant and continuous that it stops us from contemplation even for a minute. To such distraction is music used.

Gopalakrishnan smiles when I complain. He understands

and agrees. In his second feature, *Kodiyettam*, he did not use background score at all. There are other sounds though. The call of birds, the beat of drums, the noise of crackers and the sound of a moving truck are appropriately used. But there is no music in the background. Explaining this, he says, 'Since the audiences are watching the life of Sankarankutty [portrayed by Gopi], it is not good to impose upon them the image of a stereotype hero. Interestingly, those who watched *Kodiyettam* did not notice the absence of background music. This experience is an encouragement for a rethink among those who believe that music is an unavoidable factor in cinema.'

Ray after watching this work wondered whether Gopalakrishnan would in future do away with background score altogether. Ray opined that when sparingly used it could make an impact. Gopalakrishnan answered that he could find no scope for music in *Kodiyettam*. But he had used M.B. Srinivasan's score (sparingly of course) to great effect in *Swayamvaram*.

In his third film, *Elippathayam*, Gopalakrishnan used the *mizhavu*—a drum-like instrument used in Koodiyattam—to create the main background score. The beat is used dramatically in the beginning when Rajamma (T. Sarada) and Sridevi (Jalaja) are seen chasing a rat with a visibly distraught Unni (Karamana Janardhanan Nair) joining them. At the end, we hear the same beat as Unni is chased around, finally to be carried away from his home and thrown into a pond!

Gopalakrishnan believes that music need not be the only hyphen between two actions or dialogues. There are so many sounds one can use. We live among a variety of 'noises', made by automobiles, machines, people, animals and birds. The honking of a vehicle, the drone of a water pump, the laughter of men, the trumpeting of an elephant, the howling of a jackal and the cawing of crows are some of the sounds that can be used to enrich a frame and convey an idea.

Adoor gives an example: 'I was shooting the bar scene in

Swayamvaram with Viswanathan [Madhu] and the principal of a tutorial college as well as his manager [Karamana]. There are long silences between their conversations. Through these silences, the characters continued to eat and drink, making noises: the clink of glasses and the sound of drink being poured and dishes being laid on the table produced a rhythmic pattern. I preserved all this while I edited the scene, and later found that these sounds between conversations actually complemented the dialogues.

'Even silence is part of sound. It is bracketed between two spells of sound. Silence also lends greater importance to the sound that is to follow. So, it is with great care that a director must introduce sound after a period of silence,' Adoor writes in *Cinema Anubhavam*. Even in *Swayamvaram*, his first full-length venture, he appears to have accomplished the right balance of sound and silence. He avers: 'I noticed that listening is as important as viewing. The natural sounds beyond storytelling can intensify the effect of images.'

Swayamvaram was shot on real locales, and the dialogues and sound effects were recorded along with the image. Here synchronized sound might not have been possible without the portable Nagra sound recorder that Gopalakrishnan got from the United Nations International Children's Emergency Fund (UNICEF) in return for a documentary he did for the organization. N. Harikumar, sound engineer at the Chitranjali Studio in Thiruvananthapuram, says that outdoor shooting till the Nagra came on the scene was cumbersome. It had to be done with a huge recorder fixed inside an outdoor unit van. The Nagra was amazing, because it ran perfectly in sync with the camera.

In the beginning, nobody believed that the Nagra could deliver, and I suppose Gopalakrishnan proved that it could by using it and presenting the results. For the first time, one heard on the screen the sound of sea waves breaking into rocks, the 'ting-ting' of the bell in a bus and the swish of seasoning a curry! Earlier, these noises may have been recreated in a studio, but hardly ever recorded live. *Swayamvaram* created a revolution in sound and rewrote the rules.

T. Krishnanunni, chief sound engineer at Chitranjali, tells me that it was *Swayamvaram* that strengthened his resolve to go through the sound recording course at the Pune Film Institute. Till this movie opened, cinema soundtracks comprised dialogues and music, generally borrowed from theatre, and hence theatrical. Gopalakrishnan's sound track was altogether different, and this gave hope that something novel can be done with sound.

Harikumar tells me about the enormous effort that went into shooting the bus sequence in *Anantaram*: Nalini (Shobhana) gets off a bus on several occasions to meet a waiting Ajayan (Ashokan). Harikumar and his team recorded the noise of the bus coming to a screeching halt several times so as to try and make each bus scene sound completely different from the other.

Again in *Anantaram*, there is a scene of the boy Ajayan spinning to the ticking of a clock, and the tic-tac sound is gradually amplified to a theatrical level. Till, he falls down. Unlike Ghatak, Gopalakrishnan rarely used sound in this exaggerated manner.

It was Ghatak who introduced Gopalakrishnan to the creative possibilities of sound. 'I became aware of its immense potential when I watched his films and he talked about them at Pune,' Adoor says. However, Ghatak used sound quite differently; he was dramatic, and sometimes the audio he used had no one-to-one correspondence with the visuals. One can call this dissonant sound. There is, for instance, a scene in *Meghe Dhaka Tara*, where protagonist Nita (played by Supriya Choudhury) discovers that Sanat (Niranjan Roy), her beloved, has found another girl. As Nita walks down a flight of stairs, broken and dejected, one hears the sound of lashing—perhaps made by a whip.

Ghatak was a theatre person, and he used dissonant sound on the stage as well. This was considered innovative in his time. Nobody did that then. Adoor has talked about this impacting sound in *Meghe Dhaka Tara* several times to me, and I would suppose that this was one of Ghatak's works that got him interested in—even helped him realize—the potential of sound.

There is a significant scene in *Elippathayam* where an aeroplane makes a dramatic impact. As the plane flies over Unni's house, Sridevi drags Rajamma to the courtyard to show her the aircraft. We hear it, but do not see it. The second time when an aircraft flies over her home, she is alone, Sridevi having eloped with her lover. As Rajamma tries to reach out to it in the sky, she collapses in intense pain, the piercingly harsh sound of the aircraft signalling disastrous times for her.

Adoor writes a separate script for sound. And he walks miles, literally, to infuse life into this. Usually, he returns to the scenes of his celluloid action to capture the ambient sounds there. He would wait endlessly on tracks to record the hooting and hissing of the steam engine, would get drenched on the seashore trying to tape the roar of waves, would happily ignore the stench of liquor from drunken men to listen to their babble, and would hide behind the walls of tutorial colleges to get a feel of young banter.

In *Kodiyettam*, all the sounds, except the dialogues, were recorded by Gopalakrishnan. He travelled across Central Travancore for nearly three months to capture 'every bit of sound from the source'. His sound engineer, Ramachandran, merely handled the dialogues inside the studio. In fact, Gopalakrishnan did much of the work from holding the microphone to taping actual sounds. There are some great moments in this work: one of them is the movie song you hear fading in and out from wayside stalls as the lorry with Sankarankutty and the driver speeds by.

Gopalakrishnan's ear for film music is apparent. In

Mukhamukham, the conversations in the teashop are punctuated by and laced with early Tamil picture songs. *Katrinile Varum Geetham* wafts across the auditorium reminding us of M.S. Subbulakshmi's mid-1940's classic Tamil movie, *Meera*. It also had a Hindi version that introduced the singer, often referred to as India's nightingale, to North India. In *Anantaram*, it is again a popular Tamil film number that is heard in the background as a young Ajayan (Sudheesh) is playing a game, hitting the bull's eye with his darts, in a village fair. His aim is so accurate that the man who runs the game stall feels extremely uncomfortable with the lad on a winning streak.

The sound mix of the darts hitting the board, the movie song heard at a distance and of the other noises of a rural fair is fascinating. Even in music, Gopalakrishnan uses folk, classical, popular and instrumental numbers. He has mastered the art of a rare cocktail that has the right ingredients in the right proportions. One of these elements is silence, which, he says, is also the property of sound. Silence exists with sound, between sounds. Sometimes, silence accentuates sound.

12

The Other Actors

Over ten years ago, Adoor told *The Asian Age* that a 'film is not just an actor's performance. He is only one of the several elements. In fact, to a great extent, his presentation is a raw material. In the theatre, the role of an actor is important. He can improvise, and improve with each show. But in cinema his role is restricted. It can be altered, edited, abbreviated, extended, cut to pieces ... anything can be done. He is not even playing directly to the audience. He has to perform to the satisfaction and fulfillment of the director's vision of the movie.'

This holds true for humans. But, what about the rest of the cast? The 'others' who also act in a film. They are the denizens of the animal and bird kingdoms. Gopalakrishnan has little control over them, and here cinema transforms into an actor's medium. 'It is impossible to either brief them on the scene to be shot or direct them to act. Then how do we include them in cinema? It is through perseverance and patience, and occasionally by tricking them into playing the parts,' he says in *Cinema Anubhavam*.

A hard task, but he is not to be cowed by this. 'I take care to include animals or birds or even insects in my movies. Man becomes truly complete only with the interplay of life forms around him, including plants and trees. This is what makes him one with nature.

'The street cat that strolls on the roof in *Swayamvaram*, the naughty tuskers, and the black cow that chases Sankarankutty out of the shop veranda into the lashing rain in *Kodiyettam*, different kinds of dogs and the hen that lays eggs in the attic in *Anantaram*, the cranes, the crows, parrots, mynahs and a host of other birds, and the fish in the temple pond in *Vidheyan* are a few of these non-human actors which have made my films richer with their presence and histrionics.'

In *Elippathayam*, rats symbolized the decline and decay of Unni's household. Throughout the movie, their lives run parallel to those of Unni and his sister Rajamma. Gopalakrishnan conveys this with a sense of the uncanny: in the end, we see Unni being carted from his home the way his youngest sister, Sridevi, had earlier carried a rat in a trap and drowned it in a pond. Unni is thrown into the pond as well, but unlike the rat, he emerges alive.

In many ways, the rat is the protagonist, antagonist, villain, trickster and approver. It is a source of curiosity and a sign of power. The rat that seemingly turns approver by admitting to chewing Unni's shirt is blamed by his elder sister for knocking down a torch and breaking it. Here the rat changes into an actor from a mere animal.

Adoor says that it was not easy to get rats to act. Not bothered about awards and rewards, the rodents did as they pleased, and there was no question of a re-take with the same animal. Another one had to be found, and with similar features! I suppose the helmer must have become an expert on rat faces by the time *Elippathayam* was completed.

The shoot began after a large number of rats had been supplied by a professional rodent catcher, a tribal.

Gopalakrishnan did not dare to get his camera rolling before his most important actors had reported on the set! The rat-man came as well to the movie location and stayed, taking care of the nimble-footed creatures. Adoor was surprised to see the rapport he struck with them: some of them would settle on his palm to nibble at the food he would offer. Truly, the Pied Piper of Kerala.

One of the rodents was housed in a trap, and in no time it got so accustomed to living there and the routine that it would eagerly wait for food, getting a little restless every time someone passed by its cage. Indeed, when the moment came, the rat acted with panache: it is the scene where Sridevi holds up the trap for Unni to inspect. It bettered its performance when she took it to the pond to drown it. 'My heart was heavy with a feeling of guilt,' Adoor clearly remembers that day. 'I felt terrible that I was going to betray a tiny rat that had come to depend on me and the others on the set. But then the sequence could not be completed without this scene. This was a key, recurring part of the work.'

Surrounded by the crew, Sridevi walked to the edge of the pond, got down the stairs, dipped the rat-trap into the pond and held it there for a few minutes for the cinematographer Mankada Ravi Varma to freeze the act on film before the director called 'cut'. Mankada beamed. The shot had been flawless. But Gopalakrishnan was not too happy. He had killed the rodent. But as Sridevi lifted the trap out of the water, the animal stood, a little wet, but looking radiant. It seemed to be saying, 'I am ready for the next take.'

Gopalakrishnan was glad that he had not become a betrayer and murderer, and in the days after the miraculous survival, the rats and the humans developed a still closer bond. When the shoot ended, he found the rodents reluctant to go away. They must have been happy living in the midst of plenty and such amiable souls, and Gopalakrishnan must have been happier that he did not have to kill any.

His love for nature and all things natural remained undiminished, and each movie had a story within the story to say. Often, the story on the set merged with the story in the script. His scripts themselves have been liberally peppered with the elements of nature, often his own experiences with it. In *Mathilukal*, hero Basheer (Mammootty in a stellar performance) wakes up every morning in his prison cell with a smile and a greeting 'Salaam Prapanchame' (I salute you, cosmos/universe).

For this film, Thiruvananthapuram's Central Jail was replicated, at least some parts of it, inside the Chitranjali Studio. A very high wall erected to separate the prison from the world outside soon began to look so real that crows and mynahs made it their home, 'blessing it', as Adoor writes in *Cinema Anubhavam*, 'with their unrestrained droppings'.

As the principal photography progressed, and the set got crowded with men, and food flowed in large quantity, more birds appeared, though not as many as one saw in Alfred Hitchcock's 1963 film *The Birds*. The 'jail' birds were not such a horror though. Gopalakrishnan's birds were friendly, and perfectly democratic; they graciously invited dogs, mongooses, squirrels, hens, butterflies, ants and other crawlies to dinner. And they arrived in style, causing all the commotion that men learnt to cope with good-humouredly.

One late afternoon, a large murder of crows gathered on the wall. Gopalakrishnan and Mankada could not have asked for a better photo opportunity. The camera was trained on them, and the birds gave a million poses that day.

Adoor says the crows conveyed pathos, Basheer's as well, that deepened, as he grew lonelier with his friends being freed. Mynahs, on the other hand, brought optimism, and he filmed them—while they played and flitted on the wall—in sequences where freedom fighters sing songs of hope.

While the birds threw no tantrums, the squirrel that entertained Basheer had the airs of a star. Getting it to act was tough, and Mankada had to keep his camera rolling hoping to catch the squirrel as it darted out of its cage once the door opened. Attempts to guide it on a select path went in vain: nets or people blocking its path were of little use, for the animal would scamper over the net or squeeze its way through the legs. Finally, Gopalakrishnan got the shot he wanted. The squirrel went up a cashew tree, and performed, quite to its director's satisfaction.

In *Kathapurushan*, he was unlucky. His animal did not cooperate. First, the search itself for a *naden pasu* (locally bred cow) turned out to be as exhausting as David O Selznick's hunt for Scarlett O' Hara in *Gone with the Wind*. In the end, Gopalakrishnan found his Vivien Leigh in a Swiss-bred cow that could easily pass off for a *naden pasu*.

I have no idea how Vivien behaved on the set, but Gopalakrishnan's cow had made up its mind to rewrite the scene where it runs amuck frightened by the horn of an Austin car bringing in the estranged husband of Kunjunni's mother as she lay dead in the veranda. The lights were on, the sound was being recorded and the camera was rolling as the car slid into the frame and its driver honked hard hoping the cow ahead would scamper in fear. The animal was made of sterner stuff. It stood its ground, turned its head around and gave a look of utter disdain. 'What is this fuss all about?' it seemed to ask. 'No Bollywood-type histrionics for me. I am European, calm and collected. The scene has to be rewritten with my sensibilities in mind.'

Adoor called 'cut', and looked dejected. Here was a mere cow forcing him to improvise, pushing him to rewrite the scene, something no human actor would have ever dared.

That day, the cow won. Gopalakrishnan had to change the scene and re-shoot it without the cow.

13

One's Own Choice

Swayamvaram (One's Own Choice) stormed Kerala's conservative citadel of celluloid. Its plot was radical, certainly so in the early 1970s. And, synchronized sound and outdoor locales that were used here were unheard of, or almost, then in Kerala. With the help of his Nagra recorder Gopalakrishnan carried his camera beyond the studio walls to film on actual locations the story of Viswanathan and Sita, who defy their parents and elope to a city to live together—outside wedlock. This was Gopalakrishnan's first fiction feature, and it opened in 1972.

Besides real locations and live recording of sound, the movie's publicity campaign was unique. Gopalakrishnan's artist friends spent days and nights at Chitralekha drawing and painting posters for the film. Those days, cinema posters were usually designed in Chennai and printed at Sivakasi, a town in Tamil Nadu in southern India also renowned for the match and fireworks 'industry and, worse, child labour. But *Swayamvaram*'s posters were pure couture, to borrow a fashion term, each visualized, sketched and painted by artists.

Sarada, who plays Sita in the movie, was nervous when Gopalakrishnan called her for *Swayamvaram*. She was an 'outright commercial artist', as she tells me one afternoon at her bungalow in Chennai's Mahalingapuram, and was used to heavy make-up and gaudy costumes. She knew that Adoor would expect her to not just act naturally but also look natural. When he assured her that it was his responsibility to mould her into Sita she was relieved.

There are two scenes she remembers even now. One was in a bus, the opening shot, where Adoor asked her to be just another passenger. To look and behave as real people did in real buses, and for Sarada it took some courage and effort to do that. There is another scene where a pregnant Sita carries a pot of water, and 'Adoor asked me not to dramatize this. Your expression should only say this much and no more.'

In fact, the film has a series of such natural scenes. Viswanathan (Madhu) brushing his teeth; Sita picking up a bed-sheet and dropping it on the ground; a little boy sent on an errand, steering an imaginary car; the prostitute Kalyani's (Lalitha) easy charm with the smuggler Vasu (P. Venukuttan Nair) and her mocking tolerance as he appears smitten by Sita are scenes that could have been lifted from the life we see every day.

Swayamvaram is perhaps Gopalakrishnan's most conventional narrative. Its structure is simple and straightforward. The story opens with the couple who have decided to defy society, though we later see Sita in a weak moment asking Viswanathan to buy her a *mangal sutra* (wedding signet worn by married women in some parts of India) to stop idle gossip.

The movie's first scene is a long one, in a bus. The sequence introduces the two characters. Obviously they are not like the other couples and families travelling by the same bus, which is speeding towards the city (a city unfamiliar to her, not to him). All the expectations as well as the anxieties of a life ahead are written on their faces. At least a couple of passengers notice something strange about the couple.

In a way, the bus journey is a trip from illusion to reality—the reality of mundane existence in a society that is conventional, reactionary, discontent, unequal and that which provides no space for a couple who are on their own. Here the contrasts are raw and clear. Significantly, the bus scene ends at a stop signal on the road, thereby suggesting the end of dreams and fantasies. The hard and inevitable reality of existence is awaiting the couple where their idealism would be tested and possibly compromised.

Viswanathan aspires to be a writer, an occupation he hopes would help him earn money to keep his home fire burning. He goes to the publisher of a magazine to get his novel serialized. Initial encouragement from the publisher does not fructify and Viswanathan has to teach zoology in a private tutorial college, whose principal (Thikkurissi Sukumaran Nair), heavily in debt, is unable to pay him his salary or even retain him beyond a short time.

Optimism turns into pessimism as the young couple struggle to cope with the trials of life. They have to move into modest lodgings, where Kalyani is their neighbour. Sita, who is pregnant by then, is harassed by their landlord and sometimes by Kalyani's clients, including Vasu. Sita is at her wit's end, when Viswanathan is hired as a clerk in a sawmill. But his joy is short-lived, when he is accosted by a dismissed employee (Gopi). Viswanathan is troubled to find that his own placement has robbed someone else of his job.

Sita is uncomfortable pretending to be a married woman, but is not bold enough to say so. Across her street a married Kalyani cares little about community, ekes a livelihood by prostituting, has a boyfriend in Vasu and treats her husband, who comes to her begging for money to get his next fix, like dirt.

Finally, when Viswanathan, weighed down by the guilt of not being a good provider, succumbs to fever, Sita faces yet another dilemma of making a choice. Penniless and with a child to feed, she may return to her parents or become another Kalyani. Once again Sita is in a quandary, which is perhaps as disturbing as the one she was in before boarding the bus with her lover.

Swayamvaram is entrenched in its time, its pulls and pressures working on the young couple, particularly Sita. One scene clearly illuminates this: outside their hotel room, a religious procession passes by, and this seems to undermine their private space with strong moral undertones. Even Sita's almost impulsively mouthed need for a mangal sutra is indicative. The passing procession of devotees chanting prayers to the accompaniment of drums and gongs on the road below the couple's third-floor hotel room may be a normal thing in the early hours of the day. However, one cannot fail to notice an equation being drawn between the physical union of the couple and the spiritual highs. Sex and 'bhakti' afford pleasure of an indescribable kind. Note how the chanting grows louder as the sequence cuts to shots inside the room.

Exceptionally photographed by Mankada Ravi Varma—who was with Gopalakrishnan till *Nizhalkkuthu* in 2002, marking a thirty-year association that ended only because the cinematographer fell ill—*Swayamvaram* uses powerful visuals over words to tell us a love story. But the film is not just this.

Gopalakrishnan's perennial concerns about unemployment, political extremism and freedom, or lack of it, to make personal choices are addressed through Viswanathan, Sita, Kalyani and the retrenched employee. In some ways, the narrative—Shakespearean of sorts—serves to underline and highlight disturbing social issues.

If one were to look a little beyond the characters and into the frames, one would easily find a strong resonance of the 1970s' Kerala. Vishwanathan's decline and decay become the testament of his times. Forced to compromise, he joins a sawmill as a clerk, a position that is so inimical to his talent and ambition that it kills his spirit. When the dismissed employee tells him that he has robbed him of his livelihood, Viswanathan is tormented. But he has no choice, his own existence being as precarious. The employee's silent gaze into Viswanathan's eyes reminds people of a generation which had grown weary of Nehruvian idealism and Marxist ideology. The Naxalite movement, at its height in the early 1970s, finds a voice in the long speech by a leader as Vishwanathan stands in a crowd listening.

As the movie progresses, Viswanathan becomes a paradox. He is brazen enough to defy authority and tradition and live with a woman not married to him, but is yet reluctant to be part of a protest march that promises equal opportunity and, more importantly, freedom from the feudal contraptions of society. He chooses to stay away from the demonstration.

This became a talking point at the Moscow Film Festival. The Soviets could not understand why Viswanathan does not join the protest, and it later turned into official criticism.

The movie reflects the angst latent in the people of Kerala at that time. The couple's pain while they transit from a middle-class mindset to a modern ethos is a case in point.

Adoor wrote the story. It came to him quite easily. At the Pune Film Institute they had classes on script writing. Students were asked to develop a situation into a story or script with a beginning, a middle and an end. Sometimes, the professor would give them a scene from a Tagore play or novel, and at other times, a short story, and ask students to develop them into scripts. These exercises were regular affairs. But Adoor did not have to struggle, because he had been reading, writing, and producing plays, even acting in some of them, ever since he was a little boy. 'This gave me a real insight into dramaturgy. This was my big advantage,' Adoor avers. What is more, he wrote scripts for some of his classmates!

The idea of *Swayamvaram*, Adoor feels, may have been triggered by Ghatak's *Subarnarekha*, made in 1962 but released in 1965. About the tragedy of a refugee, Ishwar Chakraborty, from East Pakistan (now Bangladesh) who along with his own little sister, Sita, raises a low-caste orphan boy, Abhiram, the work is one of Ghatak's best. On the eve of Sita's marriage, she elopes with Abhiram, who is later lynched to death by a mob when he runs his bus over a child. The tragedy is compounded years later when a distraught and drunken Ishwar visits a prostitute who turns out to be Sita. Adoor says he may have been thinking of what could have happened to the couple from the moment they run away. *Swayamvaram* starts here, and sets off on a different course. Its premise is different and so are its preoccupations.

Swayamvaram ends leaving Sita with difficult choices. In a way, her dilemma reflected Gopalakrishnan's own at that point in time. 'It was about my life, my choices . . . In this film, I was probing in different directions, trying to talk about many things, such as dream and reality, hope and disenchantment, the rot in society and so on.'

Money for *Swayamvaram* came after a long struggle. Gopalakrishnan's first project, whose script was written by C.N. Sreekandan Nair, a renowned Kerala playwright, had been rejected by the Film Finance Corporation, which later became the National Film Development Corporation of India. Adoor's second effort—when he himself wrote the script—did not go in vain. The Corporation agreed to finance him, the first time it was funding a film institute graduate, and the sum was Rs 1,50,000. The rest of the money, Rs 1,00,000, was raised by the Chitralekha Film Cooperative from the marginal profits it had made from producing documentaries.

When the movie opened, it was an 'instant flop', rues Adoor. In many cinemas it did not run beyond seven days, its star material of Madhu and Sarada notwithstanding. Nobody believed that a film could work without songs and dances. It was visual and cerebral, not verbose and crass. And *Swayamvaram* did not have the comedian Adoor Bhasi, the vital box-office ingredient of those days, and it was widely perceived that no movie could work without him. It was ignored, perhaps even jeered at, at the Kerala State Awards.

However, when the National Awards were announced, they made media headlines. It clinched the *Swarna Kamal* for Best Film, and awards for Best Director, Best Cinematographer (Mankada Ravi Varma) and Best Actress (Sarada, who plays Sita). Indeed, she is called Urvashi Sarada: her first national award came for her role in Aloysius Vincent's Malayalam work *Thulabharam* (Justice) in 1968. Her third was for a Telugu film, B.S. Narayana's *Nimajjanam* (The Immersion) in 1978.

Swayamvaram was re-released. This time, everybody wanted to see it, including Gopalakrishnan's detractors, who were curious to find out what had made the jury in New Delhi applaud it. *Swayamvaram* went on to become a commercial success, and in thirty days the loan was repaid, much to the astonishment of the corporation. Perhaps for the first time, it was getting its money back with interest and on time. Chitralekha used the money the movie made to buy equipment, which was otherwise being hired. Gradually, the cooperative had a good studio and a processing laboratory.

Swayamvaram came seven years after Gopalakrishnan had passed out of the Pune Film Institute. His second work, *Kodiyettam*, came five years later, and his third, *Elippathayam*, four years after that. Long intervals between his movies became the norm. Ray once suggested that he make at least one film every year. Gopalakrishnan never did, never does—the only exception being his latest venture, *Oru Pennum Randaanum* (A Climate for Crime). He made two movies one after the other, *Naalu Pennungal* and *Oru Pennum Randaanum*. The first was released in 2007 and the second the following year.

He says he is lazy and that is why he has not made many films. Maybe that is the kind of space and time he needs to think of a good plot and write a script that satisfies him. In an important way it is the script that has the ability to make or

mar a movie. And many Indian film scripts are generally
written with very little imagination or intelligence.

Gopalakrishnan's script for *Swayamvaram* was tight, and his
lead characters were unforgettable. They were essayed by two
big stars of the day, Madhu and Sarada. Did a newcomer like
Gopalakrishnan feel intimidated by them?

'No, I had no problem directing Sarada or Madhu, because
of my theatre background. I had handled artistes, big and
small, and knew exactly what I wanted from them. Sarada
went happily through a number of rehearsals and takes. She
intuitively knew that she was improving with every take. This
is a great thing about her,' Adoor is effusive in his praise.

Artists are very intelligent people, and they sense it when
they are part of a serious, committed project. Their director
rises in their estimation when he can tell them exactly what he
wants. 'One of the things I am very particular about is the
dialogue I write. I have very few dialogues in my movies, but
whatever there are, they are very important. They cannot be
altered. They cannot be changed this way or that way just
because an actor wants it,' Adoor is firm.

'If I need to do twenty-five takes, I would very well do them.
But usually my ratio is an austere 4:1,' Adoor says. However,
he has several rehearsals before he lets the camera roll, pan
and tilt. 'When you have a particular choreography in your
mind, it has to be rehearsed and perfected. Some improvement
is possible in takes, and some at the cutting or editing stage.'

With all these—rehearsals and retakes—*Swayamvaram* was
completed in about fifty days, in two schedules. Gopalakrishnan
believes in continuous shooting, at one go, if that is possible.
This way, energy is concentrated and memory remains intact.
It is important to remember to do the right things at the right
time.

Sometimes, the right things happen by themselves at the
right time. The film's principal photography took place at the
height of summer. There was this one particular afternoon

when Adoor had planned to shoot a rain sequence, hoping a summer shower would come to his aid. There was of course no sign of rain, and the occasional clouds in the sky moved away as quickly as they had appeared. But when the crew was about to pack up for the day after taking some shots of Viswanathan sitting in his veranda, jobless and depressed, huge drops of rain fell, suddenly and unexpectedly as if Adoor's prayers had been answered. 'This was ideal for my visualization and we quickly shot the scene from all possible angles,' Adoor tells me how nature helped him that day.

There are many such interesting incidents related to the movie, giving it a life of its own—from its inception to its recognition as a major piece of artistic work.

Yet, *Swayamvaram* had the dubious distinction of being selected at the competition in Moscow, but not rewarded with a prize. Every Indian film had won an award there. When Gopalakrishnan returned home, a hostile media confronted him. *Screen* wrote that *Swayamvaram* had put India to shame. M.G. Ramachandran, a former Chief Minister of Tamil Nadu and leader of the All India Anna Dravida Munnetra Kazhagam, who was also in Moscow then planning a collaboration with the erstwhile Soviet Union, came back to Chennai and told the media that *Swayamvaram* was selling Indian poverty abroad. Ray had faced similar flak for *Pather Panchali*.

Adoor was deeply hurt, all the more so because he had helped Ramachandran translate his speech during a press conference in Moscow. The two were staying at the same hotel, and Ramachandran could not speak any language other than Tamil and Malayalam. Adoor says he had a tough time translating the flowery prose of the political leader. 'And this is how he paid me back.'

That was not the end of the film's travails. In those days, regional panels used to recommend regional movies for the National Awards. There was a panel in Chennai that previewed films in four southern languages (Tamil, Malayalam, Kannada and Telugu). This preview came on the heels of the Kerala State Awards, and there were people on the Chennai panel who were well entrenched in the Malayalam movie industry. They were not happy that younger people like Gopalakrishnan, with a degree from the Pune Film Institute to boot, were trying to become a force. They rejected *Swayamvaram*.

A distressed Adoor sent a page-long telegram (there was no e-mail those days, and no direct telephone dialling) to Ramesh Thappar, who was presiding over the National Awards Committee in New Delhi, requesting the panel to view *Swayamvaram*. Thappar was powerful, and close to Indira Gandhi.

There was no reply from Thappar.

But a wonderful news came over the radio as Adoor and his friends were having tea. For one who had little hope of his movie being recognized, it must have shaken him when he heard the radio say that *Swayamvaram* clinched the National Award for Best Film. The cable had worked, and Thappar had done justice not just to a Malayalam movie but to small, intimate and meaningful cinema. Adoor's victory that day symbolized a victory for such films.

Thappar did more. He recommended that the regional committees be abolished, and the selection process left to a single panel in New Delhi.

But *Swayamvaram* and its auteur created history in more than one way. A work without songs and dances or comedy and with rare austerity and social commitment rewrote the awards process and gave a new meaning to the business of cinema by re-running to packed houses and becoming a huge success, impacting Malayalam cinema in no small way.

SWAYAMVARAM

Cast and Credits

Year of production: 1972

Colour: Black and white

Language: Malayalam

Duration: 125 minutes

Story, Screenplay and Direction: Adoor Gopalakrishnan

Co-Scenarist: K.P. Kumaran

Producer: Chitralekha Film Cooperative

Cinematography: Mankada Ravi Varma

Music: M.B. Srinivasan

Sound: P. Devadas

Art Direction: Dathan and Sivasakthan Nair

Editing: A. Ramesan

Cast: Madhu (Viswanathan), T. Sarada (Sita), Lalitha, (Kalyani), P.K. Venukuttan Nair (Smuggler Vasu), Thikkurissi Sukumaran Nair (tutorial college principal), Karamana Janardhanan Nair (his manager)

Prizes: National Awards for Best Film, Best Direction, Best Actress (T. Sarada) and Best Cinematography

Festivals: New York, Washington, Moscow, London, Paris, Nantes, La Rochelle, Pesaro, Helsinki, Ljubljana, Munich, Fribourg and Colombo among others

Newborn Adoor on his aunt's lap. Sitting in the centre on the chair is his mother, Gauri Kunjamma. Standing on the right is his father, Madhavan Unnithan

The house at Pallickal, Adoor, where Gopalakrishnan was born

A young Adoor, 1973–74

Adoor in his middle years

Adoor with wife Sunanda

Adoor with daughter Aswati, wife Sunanda, grandson Tashi
and son-in-law Tshering

With Satyajit Ray at Padmanabhapuram Palace,
near Thiruvananthapuram

With film critic Iqbal Masud at Nantes

With writer Basheer

With director G. Aravindan, painter Viswanathan, actress Jalaja and cinematographer Mankada Ravi Varma
(L to R)

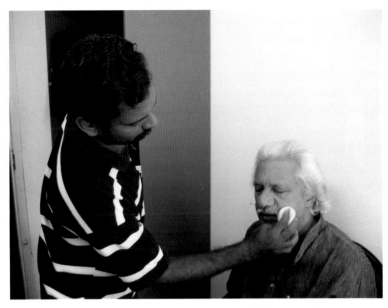

Being made up before a TV interview at Thiruvananthapuram

With cinematographer Mankada Ravi Varma at a shoot

A still from *Swayamvaram* (1972)

A scene from *Kodiyettam* (1977)

Filming *Elippathayam* (1981)

A scene from *Elippathayam*

A shot from *Mukhamukham* (1984)

A still from *Anantaram* (1987)

Coaching favourite actor B.K. Nair for *Mathilukal* (1989)
as Mammootty looks on

Shooting *Mathilukal* inside Thiruvananthapuram Central Jail
with actor Mammootty

A scene from *Mathilukal*

Patelar and Thommi in *Vidheyan* (1993)

Discussing a scene with actress Mini Nair for *Kathapurushan* (1995)

A poignant scene in *Kathapurushan*

A telling scene in *Nizhalkkuthu* (2002)

A shot from *Naalu Pennungal* (2007)

At the shoot of *Oru Pennum Randaanum* (2008) at Ambalapuzha

Adoor with Jagadeesh (L) and Sudeesh (R) on the
set of *Oru Pennum Randaanum*

A scene from *Oru Pennum Randaanum*

Shooting *Ganga* (1985), a documentary, with painter Viswanathan

Preparing a shot with Kathakali maestro Kalamandalam Ramankutty
Nair for a documentary on him in 2005

A shot from the documentary on Mohiniattam,
Dance of the Enchantress

14

The Ascent

*K*odiyettam (The Ascent) rolled out of the cans in 1977. It was even more radical than Gopalakrishnan's first feature, clearly implying that he was, like the film's title and protagonist, on the ascent. Gopi plays Sankarankutty, a rustic simpleton, enamoured of chasing kites and excited about temple festivals. His juvenility draws him to village boys, who bully him and demand his attention. His rootless life anchors, if at all, in grand rural fairs, where, in the midst of the din of drums and the light from fireworks, he finds joy. Balding and far removed from the classic celluloid hero, Gopi was Gopalakrishnan's superman, albeit in a quiet, unassuming manner. A bit of a joker, an occasional drunkard, Sankarankutty is consumed by wanderlust—much to the woe of his sister and later his wife. In Sankarankutty's unemployment there is an apparent link between *Swayamvaram* and *Kodiyettam*. But the similarities end here. While *Swayamvaram* traces the decline and decay of its lead characters, *Kodiyettam* narrates the rise of Sankarankutty. We see him develop from a bumbling bumpkin into a mature, responsible human being. 'You watch him becoming a person, becoming an individual. There is love and tragedy in his life as he becomes a full-fledged adult,' Adoor told an interviewer in 1991.

Sankarankutty's existence involves only eating, sleeping and floating around. His strange urge to flee from the first sign of permanence and fear of sharing his space with anybody else fade in as the movie unfolds. His thirst for freedom begins to look less obsessive as he comes closer to his wife, Santhamma (Lalitha), and finally in what seems like remarkable reformation, he returns to her and the two share a bashful silence before he offers her a gift. She bursts out crying, the sound of her sobbing mingles with the temple festivity in the background reaching a crescendo with the rat-a-tat of firecrackers.

The film is episodic in structure. The viewer gets the feeling of being with the character as he moves along through apparently an uneventful life, but which, in fact, culminates in the very maturing and individuation of the protagonist. Gopalakrishnan lays bare the life of a man, who plays with children, goes fishing with them, climbs trees for coconuts, eats gluttonously and drinks silly in toddy shops. He loves spectacle and space, his own. When his sister (Vilasani), who works as a maid in the city, finds him a wife, he meekly submits without even realizing what it would mean in terms of taking on responsibilities. He escapes. Disappearing from home for weeks, to the disappointment and disgust of his wife, till she, pregnant with his child, walks out of home.

When a remorseful Sankarankutty visits Santhamma at her mother's (Adoor Bhavani) house, she rebukes him for his callous ways and refuses to let her daughter go back with him. His wife is equally angry.

It is then that the movie turns a corner. Sankarankutty finds a job as an assistant to a truck driver, essayed by Aziz. On his road journeys, Sankarankutty meets the driver's mistress (Radhamani) and is appalled. However, when he meets the driver's wife and children, Sankarankutty understands the warmth and comfort of a home. He suddenly begins to miss his own wife and child.

The third and final visit he makes to Santhamma's parental home ends in reconciliation, and their joy finds an echo in the jubilation at the village, at the festival in the temple. The crackers go off. It is time to celebrate. The mood is just right. The man and the woman have come together.

Kodiyettam is a canvas of joy. It really is an ascent. *Swayamvaram* stands in contrast, where a happy couple find their lives being shattered by unemployment and poverty. In the end, the man dies, and the woman confronts a crisis.

Gopalakrishnan's second feature ran for more than 100 days in many Kerala centres. At Kottayam, it crossed 120 days. Although the producer, Chitralekha, made thirteen prints, *Kodiyettam* was initially released in only two cinemas, at Kottayam and Haripad. But when the picture picked up right from its first day, all those who had declined to screen it began having second thoughts! The word of mouth was so strong and convincing that hundreds of people flocked to see Gopalakrishnan's hero, unimpressive and ungainly to look at, but lovable.

And Sankarankutty's Gopi, walked away with the National Award for Best Actor. The movie got the Best Regional Picture Prize. This time, Gopalakrishnan's home turf did not dare ignore him: The Kerala State Awards for Best Film, Best Director, Best Actor, Best Script (Adoor Gopalakrishnan) and Best Art Direction (Sivan) went to *Kodiyettam*.

It was not an easy movie to make, says Meera Sahib, Adoor's chief assistant for the film. There were some shots that were risky and extremely difficult then. Those inside the truck driver's cabin, for instance. 'The camera was placed just outside the window, and Mankada Ravi Varma on the footboard, perilously perched, was rolling the camera.' High adventure on high roads.

Principal photography began in 1975, and the negative had to be sent to Chennai's AVM Laboratory for processing. Once processed, Gopalakrishnan had no money to pay the fee. The film lay there for a whole year, and when he returned to collect it, he found some of the rolls missing! He had to re-shoot the scenes.

The effort paid off—also because Gopalakrishnan wanted to do something innately novel here. 'I wanted to make a movie that would appear to have happened without my interference,' Adoor smiles. 'I wanted the audience to feel that nobody had "directed" *Kodiyettam*. No manipulation at any level. This is the impression I wanted to convey.'

Sankarankutty's life and the film are like a graph that charts new heights. He is introduced as a fancy-free and footloose guy. His first journeys are on foot and around his village. When he gets more adventurous and curious, and restless with the familiar, he rides a bullock-cart to travel farther. The line on the graph moves up till he gets into the truck.

This gradation also implies his growth as a man and social being. He mellows down, broods and re-examines himself. A man who had flown with the tide, allowed himself to be pushed, pulled and bullied to the extent that a false police charge had been slapped on him, pauses to ponder and examine himself. There is one revealing scene in which he begins to sport a moustache, an act that suggests the assertion of masculinity and will. With these he assumes a definite character and ceases to be one among the aimless multitude. He realizes the need for love, and to be loved.

Santhamma sees this transformation, and her acceptance of a sari from him as a gift indicates the marriage of the two minds. The union takes place to the exuberant sounds of firecrackers signifying happiness and fulfilment.

Kodiyettam's success also lay in Gopalakrishnan's ability to draw from his experiences. 'Its story emerges from my village, from the people I knew there, I grew up with,' Adoor talks about the birth of an idea that gradually developed into Sankarankutty and his story.

Gopalakrishnan knew a couple of characters like Sankarankutty, though what we see on the screen has some add-ons drawn from others. 'But there are men like him around us even today. He is not somebody entirely from the past,' Adoor is reluctant to name the men who in some ways became Sankarankutty.

'Basically *Kodiyettam* is about the individuation of a person. What happens is, we follow this man, who is just a number in the crowd. He is freely available for anybody's political procession. Only you have to pay him his wage. He is available to the village boys, who offer him companionship. He is available as a handyman to the widow (Kaviyoor Ponnamma) in his village. In return, she gives him a sumptuous meal as well as compassion and understanding apart from his wages. When she finds that she is pregnant with the school-master's [Thikkurissi Sukumaran Nair] child, the widow ends her life rather than face shame and scandal,' Adoor adds.

A time comes when Sankarankutty detaches himself from the crowd and begins to think. And thinks for himself. About himself. He becomes an individual and begins to understand that there is a self before the rest. He does not want to be part of a crowd and steps out of it.

Gopalakrishnan compares the structure of *Kodiyettam* to a temple festival, where an internal development takes place quietly and unostentatiously. Its dramatic climax is expressed outwardly through fireworks that illuminate the night sky in all their splendour. Sankarankutty's internal maturation is similarly conveyed through his concern and love for his wife. Their emotional union is matched by the display of fireworks at the temple. At some point, the festival's finale and the couple's coming together become intertwined.

Gopi was an exceptional performer, and at that point he was virtually unknown. Except for the brief part in *Swayamvaram* as the laid-off worker, he had done little else. So it was very convenient to shoot him, and Gopalakrishnan took him to temples and village festivals in interior Kerala, operating the camera himself. Although Mankada was the cinematographer, there were occasions when the director had to step in his place for want of time and money. They would suddenly hear about a festival and would have to rush there, and Mankada, who was living in Chennai, could not be had in such contingencies.

Kodiyettam was shot and completed in 1975 but was released in 1977, because Gopalakrishnan had no money to pay AVM Laboratory, where the movie was processed. Ultimately, the money from his documentary on Idukki was used for paying the laboratory fee.

Kodiyettam had no background music. 'I did not want to use any,' Adoor says. 'If you use background score, somehow it gets underlined. At least some passages do. I did not want to track it in any way. I wanted to give the feel that it was happening right there, and you, the audiences, were the fortunate ones to be taken to the place of action. So there was no manipulation, there was nobody operating the strings from behind.' Often background music is used as a tool to influence emotions. This is an easy way to grab viewer attention when the performance or the scene itself does not have enough emotional content. Gopalakrishnan never had this problem. For, the scenes and the acting in his films had adequate emotional quotient. He did not use background scores at all. But he used a whole lot of other sounds, natural sounds that suggested much more than what music could have. *Kodiyettam*'s soundtrack became very special in that sense.

Mira Binford emphasized this in a 1979 issue of *Film Comment*, where she wrote 'Gopalakrishnan's success lies also in the use of sound in a way not matched by any Indian director. The music of Kathakali, the temple orchestra, the plaintive recitations by village folk, domestic noises and sounds produced by birds, animals and a speeding lorry are all used to add a poetic effect to the movement of this feature.'

And the helmer worked hard to get the effects. He hid in a

toddy shop recording the sounds there, of men drinking and cursing one another. He went to remote villages in Central Travancore capturing the noises there, of children and adults getting together in the evening to chant hymns. '*Rama, Rama, Rama, Rama, Rama, Rama, Pahimam; Rama Padam Cherane Mukundha Rama Pahimam,*' is one such. We hear this in some other movies of his as well, *Naalu Pennungal,* for example.

There are some significant sequences in *Kodiyettam* that provide the story's vital links, and an insight into characterization. The sexual affair between the widow and the teacher is handled skilfully and with dignity. We see 'meetings' between them. Sankarankutty sees them too. On a path that cuts across a rice field, he sees the man and the woman walk towards each other. But do they stop to exchange a word or two? Sankarankutty misses that, because he is momentarily distracted by some boys who call him. By the time he turns around, they have crossed each other and are walking in different directions. Another time, he sees them in a temple, but they disappear behind a stone pillar. Yet another time, he hears them talk behind the high temple wall. It is not very clear what she is telling him, but she is weeping. Sankarankutty is perplexed. He suspects there is something between them, but is not quite sure.

Apart from them, the film is full of characters, delightful characters. The elephant keeper who hires Sankarankutty as his assistant, the man who runs the tea-shop, the woman who is in charge of a watering hole, where men assemble for a drink, and others. The elephant keeper gets drunk and tells Sankarankutty that he would like to take care of Sankarankutty's sister. The brother does not like this, gets upset and wants to stab him with a broken bottle. This scene is cut to one where we see him being tossed about in a speeding truck. He has become the truck driver's helper.

The driver is a tough guy, a hard taskmaster. There is one scene in which Sankarankutty vomits, and the driver hands him a bucket and asks him to clean it up. He spends most of his time at the wheel, stops by at his home, gives gifts to his children, tells them to study hard and leaves without even a meal. A little later, he visits his mistress, and asks Sankarankutty to sleep in the truck.

All this may seem like 'dry philosophy', but as Binford adds in the same article, 'Gopalakrishnan lifts his theme to an intense human drama, of guilt and accusation and correction and retrieval.' And this is achieved through a controlled use of the camera. The writer also says that Adoor's language is used with economy and is simple as well as metaphorical. There is a mix of realism and deeper poetic quality of life around us to satisfy both the artistic and the thematic demands of the work.

'No other kind of treatment would have been proper for the movie,' Adoor avers. 'A more stylish approach would have seemed like condescension, of looking down upon Sankarankutty. On the other hand, if I had made him a hero one would have had to look up towards him. Both were unsuitable.' So, Gopalakrishnan decided to maintain his perspective on the level of the eye of his protagonist.

Kodiyettam was the first work of Gopalakrishnan that Ray saw. He was laughing throughout, and enjoyed it immensely. But he missed the music, and said that if used sparingly it could become very powerful. But nobody else missed the background score. Gopi did not let anybody miss that. It was a performance par excellence. But a helmer other than Gopalakrishnan might not have been able to draw such brilliance from Gopi, at least in the actor's early career.

Yet, the two never worked together again.

KODIYETTAM

Cast and Credits

Year of production: 1977

Colour: Black and white

Language: Malayalam

Duration: 128 minutes

Story, Screenplay and Direction: Adoor Gopalakrishnan

Chief Assistant: Meera Sahib

Producer: Chitralekha Film Cooperative

Cinematography: Mankada Ravi Varma

Sound: Adoor Gopalakrishnan (Effects), Ramachandran

Art Direction: Sivan

Editing: M. Mani

Cast: Gopi (Sankarankutty), Vilasani (Sankarankutty's sister), Lalitha (Santhamma), Adoor Bhavani (Santhamma's mother), Thikkurissi Sukumaran Nair (school-master), Aziz (truck driver), Radhamani (truck driver's mistress)

Prizes: National Awards for Best Regional Film and Best Actor (Gopi); Kerala State Awards for Best Film, Best Direction, Best Screenplay, Best Actor (Gopi) and Best Art Direction

Festivals: New York, Washington, London, Paris, La Rochelle, Nantes, Helsinki, Berlin, Munich, Pesaro, Ljubljana, Fribourg, Adelaide and Tunis among others

15

The Rat-Trap

*E*lippathayam (The Rat-Trap) set Gopalakrishnan free. It provided a great deliverance for him. The post-*Kodiyettam* years saw him disillusioned with Chitralekha, the baby he created with such care. It had produced his first two films. No more, he decided. He wanted to make cinema outside the cooperative. He himself had little money. But it came from a man of business to the core who saw the spark of brilliance in Gopalakrishnan and the value of promoting meaningful cinema. He was K. Ravindranathan Nair of General Pictures. People call him Ravi, but is better known as Cashew Ravi. He has a flourishing business in the cash crop that he inherited from his family. But often his passion for movies was stronger than his love for the kernel.

Ravi had been watching the young Gopalakrishnan ever since he stepped out of Pune. Ravi followed *Swayamvaram* and *Kodiyettam*, even though he was busy producing G. Aravindan's *Kanchana Seeta* (The Golden Substitute) in the late 1970s, when Gopalakrishnan's Sankarankutty was taking Kerala by storm.

After *Kodiyettam*, Gopalakrishnan found himself in a vacuum. He had distanced himself from Chitralekha and there were no funds to make his next film. That is when he met Ravi. Their association saw them through four movies: *Elippathayam*, *Mukhamukham*, *Anantaram* and *Vidheyan*. The relationship worked splendidly, because Ravi gave his director a free hand; he would visit the set just once for the *mahurat* or the opening ceremony. And hardly ever after that.

Gopalakrishnan, on his part, was not only methodical and dedicated, but also made sure that his producer got his money back, preferably with a profit. Ravi liked this commitment. He tells me at his palatial and tastefully decorated bungalow at Kollam that of all the four films, *Elippathayam* remains his favourite, an all time best. 'It is closest to my heart,' and documents in all its starkness the feudal life in Kerala, and its decline.

In many ways, *Elippathayam*, released in 1981, is the finest work in Gopalakrishnan's repertoire. It was his first work in colour, and it engaged me with its rich visuals, riveting narrative style and outstanding performances. I am not surprised that when it was shown at the Cannes Film Festival in 1982, Mrinal Sen, who was on the main international jury that year, remarked that he would have voted for *Elippathayam* had it been in the competition.

It was not, and I suppose the Europeans as usual got a little muddled with Gopalakrishnan's storytelling ways, not always simple to understand and sometimes requiring more than one viewing for fuller and deeper appreciation.

The *Sight and Sound* critic John Gillet wrote in the International Film Guide that *Elippathayam* 'is a rarity in Indian cinema in that its formal methods and visual styling become the primary tools in tracing this study of paranoia. Utilizing minimum dialogue, Gopalakrishnan builds a structure of closely interlinked images with extreme concentration on shot details—the house's veranda, open doors, pots, water-drenched street, hands and eyes.'

Elippathayam's Unni, played by Karamana Janardhanan Nair in probably his life's best role, is a middle-aged, greying, selfish man representing a disintegrating feudal order. He remains unaffected and unmoved, even disdainful, of the socio-economic changes around him. These have altered equations between classes even in remote villages, but Unni clings to his private space in his ancestral house, stepping out but rarely. He keeps away from women and sex. Wimpish in character, he takes to his heels at the slightest suggestion of sex from a woman. There is a wonderfully illustrative scene in a cashew grove, where Unni is accosted by a working-class woman, who is apparently attracted to him. The man cowers. In another scene, Unni is seen walking to a wedding, but midway he finds he cannot cross a small puddle. He returns home without attending the ceremony. In yet another instance, he refuses to budge from his bed in the middle of the night when coconut thieves are out there in his grove.

Unni resides in his ancestral house with two of his younger sisters, Rajamma (essayed by T. Sarada) and Sridevi (Jalaja). His elder sister, Janamma (Rajam K. Nair), is married and lives away, but asserts her right over her share of the family property. Unni is reluctant to part with this, perhaps fearing a fall in his own living standards.

Rajamma is into her late thirties, docile and slavishly attached to Unni, who uses and exploits her, turning down one marriage proposal after another for her under some pretext or the other. She toils for him the whole day, looking after the needs of a man who does not lift a finger to help her. When a cow strays into their front courtyard, it is Rajamma who has to hurry from the kitchen at the far end of the house to chase it away. Unni's responsibility begins and ends with a call to her. He does not even heat his own bath water.

Insensitive to the core and lethargic to the point of appearing ridiculous, Unni is a classic icon of a parasitic familial system that lives on others' labour. Loath to take on anything that he perceives as liability, he appears unaffected even by Sridevi's elopement presumably with her college lecturer.

Finally, caught between a decadent past and an inhospitable and inconvenient present, Unni crumbles when Rajamma falls seriously ill. Incapable of facing life, let alone doing even routine chores, he withdraws like a rat into a hole. Guilty and isolated, he becomes paranoid.

The movie ends dramatically: Unni is forced out of the room where he had shut himself, carried to the village pond and thrown into it. He rises out of the water looking like a rat, all wet and shaken. A simile is apparent here to the earlier scenes of Sridevi carrying a rodent in a trap and drowning it in the pond. However, unlike the four-footed creature, Unni emerges from the water. Has he got a new lease of life shorn of feudalistic excesses? The film, like *Swayamvaram*, ends with a teaser. It is for us, the viewers, to wrack our brains and come up with answers. The climax lends itself to debate.

Elippathayam is Gopalakrishnan's most poetic expression that examines human ties in a dying social structure. This is presented through disquieting episodes. Rajamma's deep anguish at such monumental neglect of her by Unni is one. The yearning for love and life translates into severe abdominal pain. Unni is full of himself: this self-absorption is effectively shown in a lengthy shot of him trimming his moustache. Later, he clips his finger nails, and looks worried when he sees a drop of blood on his finger tip, a concern that he reserves for himself. He has no space for others, and is always engaged with himself.

In Unni and his disdain for and indifference to the world around him, in Sridevi and her own brand of narcissism, in Janamma and her utter lack of sympathy for Rajamma, and in Rajamma herself and her sickening servility we see a horrible state of stagnation and the decline of a once flourishing class.

One of the most disturbing features of this movie is the power Unni exerts over Rajamma. Here is a man who comes from a set-up where political power sanctioned abusive authority. When this power disappears, the home becomes a convenient ground for the exercise of such offensive control: Unni's terrifying hold over Rajamma is a case in point. The old master–subject power equation transforms into another form of power dynamics, that of man–woman. Rajamma being weak and accommodating is ideal for a bully like Unni, who dare not impose his will on the stronger members of his family.

Here, in *Elippathayam* too, like in his earlier works, an autobiographical element creeps in. Adoor says, 'When I shot the film, feudalism was already over. I saw it coming to an end in the 1940s when I was a child. I watched the process of dissolution and reorganization. But I showed the progression differently in my work.'

Along with feudalism, the matrilineal system too was crumbling as Gopalakrishnan was growing out of his shorts. More and more people were marrying outside their families. The custom of a man, for example, marrying his maternal uncle's daughter was disappearing with the advent of education and medical science that said consanguineous sexual relationships could result in unhealthy children and greater incidence of hereditary diseases in them.

In *Elippathayam*, Janamma marries outside her family and lives with her husband. Tradition required the woman to marry within the clan and her husband to stay with her in her family house. When she asks Unni for her share of the ancestral property, he refuses, though he is supposed to provide for his sisters and their children. The uncle was more important to a child than its own father in matrilocality.

Soon after Gopalakrishnan completed *Elippathayam*, he said that of the three pictures he had directed till then, his latest was the one he loved most dearly. He had created his own family background in it, or almost. Unni's house was akin to the one Gopalakrishnan grew up in at Adoor. There were other similarities, including characterizations and situations.

However, he feels that though it may be very well to connect a work of art to a personal experience, one should never imagine it being replicated, at least immediately. The actual source of inspiration/experience should necessarily go through a process of creative/imaginative transmutation.

Gopalakrishnan is known to occasionally model his characters on those he has known. 'But they are never exact replicas. If you expect that you can go wrong,' he sounds a note of caution. Unni was in some respects like Gopalakrishnan's uncle, Raghavan Unnithan. But Unni was also unlike Raghavan Unnithan in several other aspects. This is where reels roll beyond the real. Art may draw inspiration from life, but a true artist lets his imagination take over, and goes beyond to present characters that may only vaguely resemble those he would have come across. Perhaps, what we see on Adoor's screen is an intriguing collage of many real people and incidents transmuted in his mind.

He says *Elippathayam* started from a simple thought. Why is it that we do not react naturally to things around us? Probably because it is inconvenient. The inconvenience may be minor or inconsequential, but we would still wish it away. When we have a full meal, we tend to forget those who may not be able to afford it. 'It is not because we are cruel or unconcerned,' says Adoor, 'but we think that by taking cognizance of it, we would let ourselves be bothered.'

As the film shooting began and progressed, Gopalakrishnan's detailing became apparent. The art director Sivan, who lives in Haripad, tells me that his director called him one evening with a terse instruction for the next day's shoot of *Elippathayam*. 'Sivan, I must have a tender areca nut tree with a pepper plant tomorrow morning. It must have bunches of pepper . . . At any cost.' Sivan was in a fix. It was not the season for pepper, and where was he going to find a plant with pepper on it.

That must have been Sivan's lucky day, for, against all hope, he found a bushy pepper plant that must have made a rare off-season appearance only to please Gopalakrishnan and help him in his quest for authenticity. It was a twenty-foot-high plant, whose owner thought that Sivan must be mad when he offered him Rs 500 (a huge amount for a pepper plant in the 1980s). Sivan scooped the plant out of the earth with its roots and transported it to the movie set.

For Gopalakrishnan, casting is another vital element of good cinema. 'I always look for an actor only after I complete my script. My actor has to look my character. Half my job is then done.'

Take Karamana. He looked like Unni, who had been pampered and not gone through life's hardships. This meant he did not have a proper perception of the pain and suffering of others. Physiognomy of a person is as important as his or her ability to act. He cast Sarada in *Swayamvaram*, also because she looked right for the part. Her age was right too. She looked Sita, Adoor remarks. And he got a moving performance from her, even though most of her roles till then had been loud and melodramatic.

Adoor is very particular that an actor must submit himself totally to him. This is the best way one can hope for a fine piece of acting. This is why he never discusses his script with his actors, let alone show it to them. His daughter, Aswati, says that once he begins to write a script, even she is not allowed to enter his study. The only exception is her mother, Sunanda, who gets to read the script before anybody else does.

Gopalakrishnan's control over his production is admirable. He plans meticulously, and executes his ideas even more carefully. His thoughtful use of colour, for one, in *Elippathayam* is much talked about. The three sisters were given three primary colours. Sridevi wears red, for vitality and non-conformism. She has a rebellious streak in her, the urge to live the way she wants to. Rajamma dons blue, the colour of kindness, big-heartedness and also doom. The eldest, Janamma, dresses in green for practicality and earthiness. The three primary colours when mixed become white, and Unni gets to wear white shirts with vertical lines that signify restlessness. He is afraid of everything and it includes cold water, a tiny cut, puddle on the path, sex and commitment. The lighting too was so devised to enhance and emphasize the intricacies of the work's layered sensitivities.

Sound has been used as an important dramatic element. The sound of the door opening and closing is also used for the opening and closing of the rat-trap. The creaking noise of the doors in Unni's house is metaphorical: it conveys a feeling of being trapped within the claustrophobic social milieu. The sound of the doors eerily equates the trap with the house, predicting tragedy. The beat of the *mizhavu* is in some way scary, almost heart stopping, and adds to the prevailing mood of unease and gloom. And when the sound rises in a crescendo, the accompanying visuals accentuate this terrible feeling. The noise of the aircraft heightens the effect, adding to the excruciating pain which Rajamma suffers as a plane passes over their house.

After the film was screened in Kolkata, Mrinal Sen came out of the cinema and asked Adoor whether he too had felt such pain when he had shot *Elippathayam*. 'Did you go through a terrible period in your life?' Sen had wanted to know. Adoor was surprised and asked him, 'But Mrinalda, how did you know that?'

The pain was caused by Chitralekha, which once gave Gopalakrishnan such joy. Between 1965 and 1980, he was so engrossed in nurturing Chitralekha that he had just made two movies. But then like many institutions in India, Chitralekha fell victim to power play. The stab came from behind, and Gopalakrishnan, who had spent the best part of his youth developing Chitralekha into an amazing organization, resigned. And so did Meera Sahib.

Adoor was devastated, and he tells me that had he not made *Elippathayam* then, he could have gone mad. So terrible was his disappointment and depression. He focussed all his attention and expended all his energy on the film. He tired himself physically. All in an effort to put Chitralekha behind. Such pain, I suppose, lent to the movie's intensity.

The British Film Institute honoured it in 1982 for being the 'Most Original and Imaginative Work'. It clinched the National Awards for the Best Regional Film and Best Audiography. The Kerala State Awards for the Best Film, Best Cinematography and Best Audiography also went to *Elippathayam*.

It was recently released on DVD in the UK, the second time Gopalakrishnan's work appeared in this format (*Nizhalkkuthu* was the first). Hopefully, many more of his works would be available on disc.

I feel that apart from its great qualities, the movie connected with people, like any other art form. Even Beethoven needed appreciation. Otherwise, music becomes noise.

But not everybody can be touched in the same way, as we shall see in the following chapter.

ELIPPATHAYAM

Cast and Credits

Year of production: 1981

Colour

Language: Malayalam

Duration: 121 minutes

Story, Screenplay and Direction: Adoor Gopalakrishnan

Chief Assistant: Meera Sahib

Producer: Ravi, General Pictures

Cinematography: Mankada Ravi Varma

Music: M.B. Srinivasan

Sound: Devadas

Art Direction: Sivan

Editing: M. Mani

Cast: Karamana Janardhanan Nair (Unni), T. Sarada (Rajamma), Jalaja (Sridevi), Rajam K. Nair (Janamma)

Prizes: National Awards for Best Regional Film and Best Audiography; Kerala State Awards for Best Film, Best Cinematography and Best Audiography; British Film Institute Award for the most original and imaginative film of 1982

Festivals: Cannes, Paris, La Rochelle, Nantes, Pesaro, Munich, Ljubljana, London, Washington DC, Chicago, Seattle, Houston, New York, Hawaii, Alexandria, Sao Paulo, Sydney and Melbourne

16

Face to Face

Mukhamukham courted controversy. Of the most virulent kind. The film opened in 1984 in a Kerala where politics was big business—and even big entertainment. Then, and even now. And, everybody watched everybody, and the state being small this was not difficult. It happens even now. And Gopalakrishnan was well known by then. He was three features old when *Mukhamukham* (Face to Face) began its run. It was at once perceived as an anti-Communist movie and severely panned, and, strangely, much of the criticism was sparked by a simple human behaviour. The protagonist, Sreedharan (essayed by P. Gangadharan Nair), turns an alcoholic in the second half of the film. So what, one may ask. Millions around the world get addicted to something or the other. Yes, but the Communists did not want Sreedharan to be a drunkard. For, he was not just a party cadre, but also a trade union leader on screen. That, the Communists felt, was bad publicity for a people's movement like theirs!

There were murmurs about *Mukhamukham* even while it was being shot. The members of the Congress Party in Kerala were happy, because they thought that Gopalakrishnan was making an anti-Communist movie, although they really had no clue about what was happening on the set. The Communists, on the other hand, claimed they liked the director, but would oppose his work. They had no idea either.

When the film finally opened, a Leftist friend of Gopalakrishnan said after watching it that he could be pardoned only if he excised the drinking scenes. Adoor says his friend completely missed the point. The movie would lose its meaning and essence if some parts were to be added or subtracted.

The Marxist leader and literary critic P. Govinda Pillai was quoted in an article in *The Illustrated Weekly of India* of 3 March 1985, '*Mukhamukham* is full of major historical inaccuracies. When a party leader goes underground, he maintains his links with the party. In fact, it is the party that decides that he should go underground and provides him with a safe shelter. But Sreedharan is not in touch with his party. No one knows where he is during the ten years he goes missing. This is simply not the way it happens.'

Pillai rued that there were other absurdities. No memorial had ever been erected for a Communist before verifying his death. No degenerate Communist had ever been honoured. These were terrible mistakes, and history did not support any of Gopalakrishnan's contentions.

At times, the condemnation became abusive. Adoor wrote in *Cinema Anubhavam*, 'A drunkard came to my house one day and hurled insults at me. He left after threatening to kill me for daring to make a picture "against the Communists". So, I believe I was close to becoming the first martyr to the cause of cinema.'

Paradoxically, *Mukhamukham* was seen as pro-Communist abroad and anti-Communist at home! In New York, London and Locarno, audiences and critics hailed Gopalakrishnan as a friend of the Left. In Kerala and elsewhere in India, he was its enemy. Adoor merely concludes, 'Cinema really takes place in the mind of a viewer.'

Yet, Adoor says he has been true to history and facts. 'I have studied the lives and works of a number of people who have been in the Communist movement.' Though he has not modelled Sreedharan on any one person, he certainly knew men like his protagonist, men who closely resembled him. Gopalakrishnan has seen Communists who drank and got drunk. Admittedly, he has also come across Gandhians who would picket toddy shops during the day, and return to the same shops at night and spend their pension money downing cheap country liquor!

Interestingly, soon after it opened, Gopalakrishnan got letters from many Communists living outside Kerala who said his work did not contain anything that was untrue. They quoted examples from their own lives to buttress this point. Some were bitter about the tyrannical hegemony over the individual within the party. Some complained that the party used violence to enforce loyalty or resolve political issues. There was one letter that described in graphic detail the persecution of a party worker who had angered a Marxist leader.

It was even more reassuring when Sreedharan came to Gopalakrishnan's home one morning. Or, a man who looked strikingly similar to his protagonist. He proved the critics wrong. Adoor says when he saw him at his front door, he realized that his 'character' had come visiting him. The man had not seen *Mukhamukham*, but he did not need to do that, for the story of Sreedharan was his own. A patient of tuberculosis, he was persistently coughing, asked Gopalakrishnan for some money and clothes, and said like Sreedharan he had been a true Communist. The man said he was tortured by the police, had lived underground for long periods and had had no life of his own.

Gopalakrishnan disagrees with all those who describe *Mukhamukham* as a political work. It is 'more humanist, less political'. He wrote in *Cinema Anubhavam*, 'I had portrayed Communist workers as they are—that is men with the same emotions and weaknesses of fellow human beings, and I had never intended to defame or misrepresent the movement.'

The central character happens to be a Communist, but his behaviour is not necessarily a reflection on the Communist movement.

In an interview to *Filmfare* in 1985, he reacted even more strongly to his work being political: 'I do not pretend to be a political moviemaker at all. In a political film, you have to take a stand, and fight out of commitment, all at the expense of turning blind to other aspects. As a conscientious director, I cannot say I am not affected by things political. Still, I cannot be devoured by them. I have admired people not only in the Communist movement but also in other political struggles.'

Gopalakrishnan has never been a political activist. He had his political views, though. Even in his student days, he kept himself away from political factions. In any case, campuses in the 1950s were not as politically active as they were later, say in the 1970s. And his family was hardly political. Except for his uncle Madhavan Unnithan, who was a member of Kerala's first Legislative Assembly, none from Gopalakrishnan's clan entered politics. Radio, newspapers and magazines and writings on and by Karl Marx, Vladimir Lenin and other political leaders, not necessarily Communist, were his sources of political information and knowledge. Marx and Lenin were compulsory reading at school, and Gopalakrishnan brushed up on them before making *Mukhamukham*, which endeared him to many.

Gopalakrishnan had his supporters and fans, and some of them were powerful, their power flowing out of the clatter of their typewriter keys. Iqbal Masud, the *Indian Express* movie critic, argued: 'This is the first attempt in our cinema to get inside the situation of a willed and committed revolutionary and to depict with masterly imagination and invention what happens there under the duress of a harsh and interminable battle against a formidable system.'

Across the seas from where Masud lived and worked, Mumbai, *The Guardian*'s cinema critic Derek Malcolm wrote, 'The film is not only a deeply personal statement but an intensely introspective one. It has of course been seen as some sort of indirect criticism of the Communist Party, though it is nothing of the sort. What is so impressive about it is not only its original subject matter but also the fastidious style with which it is made.'

Mukhamukham's Sreedharan comes back to his native town after a decade. He had been a Communist trade union leader, a hero to his co-workers in the factory where he laboured and a beloved of the young and old outside his workplace. However, he returns as a ghost of his former self and heads to the liquor den. When he is not drunk, he is sleeping, and his almost cadaverous form worries his folks at first. His old comrades too are amused and then disgusted. A point comes when he becomes the ridicule of the community: children throw stones at him and adults avoid him.

The two sides of Sreedharan are dealt with in two separate parts, divided by a narrative crisis, that of the mysterious death of the factory owner in 1955. This creates an even greater police repression in Kerala, where the Communist Party of India was almost shackled. Many party leaders, including Sreedharan, go underground. Ten years later in 1965, he returns to the home of his mistress, Savitri (Kaviyoor Ponnamma), a pale shadow of his former disciplined self, a great leader to his exploited men and their suffering families.

It is this Sreedharan, strong and dedicated to the cause of his fellow workers and community, that people remember—a memory that bridges the intervening decade of his unexplained disappearance.

Many changes occur in the ten years: The Communist Party wins the 1957 elections in Kerala, the first time ever in India or anywhere else a Leftist group comes to power through the ballot. A little later, the party splits into two. When Sreedharan returns, the people seek him out, the memory of an upright leader who had shrugged off pain after a brutal police beating still fresh in their minds. At a punishing hunger strike, he had once remained undaunted.

But the mystery and enigma of Sreedharan persists. He is seen burning letters, maybe sensitive party communication or letters from his wife back home. He drinks but on the sly, and lives with a woman. He does not marry her, and even has a son by her. This could have been the pre-disappearance Sreedharan.

Again, all these may not be true for they are reconstructed by people whose perception may be incorrect or clouded by hearsay. *Mukhamukham* constantly taunts us through hope and disappointment, through light and darkness. Some moments seem clear, some obscure. And then we are led into a state of confusion that clears a little later.

'*Mukhamukham* is about such ambiguities; here the untruth mirrors the truth, reality transforms into illusion,' writes Shampa Banerjee in her introduction to the movie's script (*Face to Face*). We see more of this contradiction, and in the end we seem to know so little about Sreedharan—unlike Unni in *Elippathayam*. Unni is examined literally under a microscope, the tiniest of pores on his skin clearly visible. But Sreedharan remains a riddle long after *Mukhamukham* ends. This is against the conventional notion of characterization, which is to let the audience know everything about the protagonist. This goes against the accepted norms of dramaturgy. We are kept away from the real Sreedharan. We do not know who he is.

The Sreedharan who returns shatters the image of a man who had cared little for creature comforts and whose charisma and verbal charm had overawed his community. But that man now drinks himself to stupor and is quiet, almost insolently silent, most of his waking hours.

Obviously, this Sreedharan is scary, and those who once knew him are anxious. They desperately try to match this present Sreedharan with the one in the past, who in the first place could have been a myth. What worries them even more and angers them is that this present Sreedharan mirrors their own limitations and failings. The party is divided, and some of its trusted lieutenants have begun to lead a life of debauchery. There is a scene where a trade unionist (Karamana Janardhanan Nair) invites Sreedharan home and offers him foreign liquor.

The one man who is genuinely distressed and disappointed is Sudhakaran (Ashokan), who as a boy (Viswanathan) idolized Sreedharan, and it is in this discontent that we see what Gopalakrishnan wants to say. The horrible fall of a man, and should one read in this a hidden message: Gopalakrishnan was perhaps talking about the degeneration of the Communist movement. Maybe in an indirect way, but this is never overtly conveyed. And this is never central.

The film opens with a sequence of industrialization. This came a hundred years late to India and galvanized workers into unions, which helped them fight for their rights. The opening titles are displayed against the scene of a boat taking clay to a factory. A little later, the camera enters the factory to show us tiles being manufactured. From the red-hot kiln, the shot cuts to the red flag as Communist slogans rent the air. There is Sreedharan, the firebrand leader of the trade union, commanding the love and respect of his comrades, leading a bitter and uncompromising strike in the factory.

In the first part, Sreedharan is progressively built through the memory of the people who knew him. They were comrades, admirers, critics and opponents. The second part is pure surmise: this Sreedharan who returns after his long absence is constructed through conjectures. Ultimately, history, memory, fiction and reality are mixed to create the intricate structure of the movie. This is how Sreedharan is moulded, through the reminiscences of various people he had been associated with, through their introspections and recollections and through the photographs of and documents on him. Sreedharan emerges as sheer enigma.

Adoor contends that it was to create such a puzzle that he chose Gangadharan to play Sreedharan. He had a prominent squint that made him look mysterious. And he was low-key. Real revolutionaries do not look like firebrands, and if *Mukhamukham* did not reveal his background, this was deliberate. 'I wanted him to be a riddle,' Adoor adds.

Ten years later, when Sreedharan returns to Savitri, he is a tired man. He certainly does not want to be a hero or serve the party any longer. His role as a party member is over. He indulges in drinking and sleeping, but those around him are appalled. They cannot let a once-upon-a-time hero fall to pieces. They are upset, even shattered, and probably consider this Sreedharan as a blot on the party. So, he is murdered.

Sreedharan does not get a second chance like Unni in *Elippathayam*. Or does he? He is declared a martyr. The two factions of the Communist Party come together to march in a procession carrying placards of Sreedharan's picture. The fallen hero rises again, like Unni. But this time, Gopalakrishnan's protagonist is mere cardboard.

MUKHAMUKHAM

Cast and Credits

Year of production: 1984

Colour

Language: Malayalam

Duration: 107 minutes

Story, Screenplay and Direction: Adoor Gopalakrishnan

Chief Assistant: Meera Sahib

Producer: Ravi, General Pictures

Cinematography: Mankada Ravi Varma

Music: M.B. Srinivasan

Sound: Devadas

Art Direction: Sivan

Editing: M. Mani

Cast: P. Gangadharan Nair (Sreedharan), Kaviyoor Ponnamma (Savitri), Karamana Janardhanan Nair (trade unionist), Viswanathan (Sudhakaran Junior), Ashokan (Sudhakaran Senior)

Prizes: National Awards for Best Direction, Best Screenplay, Best Audiography and Best Regional Film; Kerala State Awards for Best Film, Best Direction, Best Cinematography, Best Audiography and Best Editing; FIPRESCI (International Critics) Prize for the Best Film, International Film Festival of India, New Delhi, 1985

Festivals: New York, Washington, London, Locarno, Brussels, Antwerp, Munich, Fribourg, Manosque, Paris, Nantes, La Rochelle, Pesaro Helsinki, Ljubljana, Alexandria, Hong Kong and New Delhi among others

The work had the rare distinction of being chosen to be exhibited in the Golden Age Film Festival in Brussels as an original and innovative cinematic essay and acquired by the Royal Belgian Film Archive to be preserved for the next 400 years.

17

Monologue

Anantaram (Monologue) found voice in 1987. Unlike *Mukhamukham*, *Anantaram* caused little unease. It attracted no abuses, no brickbats, only heaps of praise. It travelled to festivals in Venice, Karlovy Vary, La Rochelle, Nantes, Amiens, Riga, London, New York, San Francisco, Hawaii and others. And it won several accolades, including the FIPRESCI Prize at Karlovy Vary, the National Awards for Best Direction, Best Screenplay and Best Audiography and the Kerala State Award for Best Direction.

In almost every way, *Anantaram* differed from *Mukhamukham*. I rummaged through heaps of material to find some similarity between the two, and, yes, I did manage to find one. Like Sreedharan, Ajayan (the *Anantaram* hero, enacted by Ashokan) met Gopalakrishnan late one evening to tell him how his life resembled the screen protagonist's. The young visitor had seen *Anantaram* a dozen times and every scene seemed to have been lifted from his own life. It could well have been a biography of his.

The youth was merely reaffirming a classic point about

Adoor's cinema. That it was real, and mirrored life in all its intriguing intensity. His characters could be an Ajayan, a Sreedharan, a Sankarankutty or a Viswanathan, and these men are those whom we pass by on the streets. Only that we seldom notice them, and we need a Gopalakrishnan to blow them up on the screen for us to sit up, take note of and get involved in their relationships, their experiences, their joys and their sorrows.

Anantaram, however, goes beyond all these. It is not just a descriptive story of a young man or his experiences and relationships. It probes the innermost recesses of his mind, and tries to examine the link between him and the community he grows up to live in. In some ways, it is a tragic tale of disorientation and disillusionment: Ajayan is a prodigy whom nobody wants to recognize. He is discouraged. His elder stepbrother, Balu (Mammootty), makes a damning statement— though in disappointment, not in anger or malice—that it would have been good for Ajayan if he had been hardworking like him, rather than brilliant. When Ajayan is not discouraged, he is cheated. There is a telling scene on the school playfield, where the young Ajayan wins a running race, but is nonetheless disqualified by his sports master on a flimsy technical ground. In a class full of mandans or duds, the teacher acknowledges Ajayan's brilliance, but grudgingly. Outside school at the village fair, his accurate aim in a game of darts and winning streak irritate the stall-keeper. He does not want the boy to take away all his earnings. So he roughs him up and warns him never to return for the game. A shaken Ajayan leaves.

Ajayan's intellect and multifaceted talents camouflage schizophrenia. (Does a gifted mind often fall prey to this mental illness? I wonder. An example that comes readily to my mind is the mathematical wizard John Nash, whose lifelong struggle with schizophrenia was made into a gripping celluloid work by Ron Howard in 2001. Also, I remember some people from my childhood, people who were extremely brainy, but eventually suffered from this debilitating mental illness.) Over a period of time, Ajayan finds that he cannot distinguish between fact and fiction: his beautiful sister-in-law, Suma (Shobhana), transforms into Nalini in his hallucinating mind. (Or, is she really Nalini, a Suma look-alike?) She becomes his love, till he accuses her of infidelity, cheating on Balu. Ajayan loses interest in life, misses his college lectures and lies about in his unkempt hostel room. He appears shabby and disinterested, his eyes often bloodshot.

Anantaram is truly a monologue 'that operates at three levels, that of experience, the memory of that experience and, finally, the rendering of that experience'. In the first part of the narrative, Ajayan tells us that he has been wronged by a society that does not comprehend brilliance. So he withdraws, and lapses into fantasies.

The movie opens in a hospital ward to the bawling of a baby. It has been abandoned by its mother, and the chief doctor (N.B. Thampi) there is so moved that he decides to bring up the child as his own son. Ajayan grows up in a hostile environment, where he finds that his talents in class, on the field and elsewhere are so envied that he remains friendless. Balu, though much older to him, is closest to him, but there is always a distance between the two. Perhaps, the difference in age or lineage impedes closer bonding. Ajayan's brief infatuation with an older girl is nipped in the bud by two bullies, and this probably deepens his hatred for 'the woman who forsook him'. His rejection and isolation seem complete when the news of his foster father's death is deliberately conveyed late so that Ajayan living away in the college hostel misses the last rites. Balu says that this was done to avoid embarrassment in the larger family.

This at once throws up a question. Was Ajayan really the doctor's foster son? Or, was he the illegitimate child of the doctor? If so, who was Ajayan's mother? Was she the mother (Kaviyoor Ponnamma) at the ashram? When the boy Ajayan is ill with typhoid, she visits him, and, bending over his feverish body, weeps. Why does she do this?

Gopalakrishnan loves to intrigue us with such puzzles, hold our attention through stimulating narrative. His cinema encourages us to participate. There are times when you want to jump off your seat and get into the frame of happening. When you watch an Adoor work, you want to contemplate, put on your thinking cap. In short, it mesmerizes your mind, boxes your brain into action.

Ajayan's psychiatric problems surface soon after Balu's marriage to Suma, and the story takes a new turn. Ajayan finds himself drawn to Suma. He writes a letter to Balu professing his love for Suma. A little later, when we are told that this is fantasy, we realize that Ajayan is hallucinating.

The second part takes us back to his childhood, where he lives with three elderly servants, his foster father and Balu invariably out of home most of the time. These three men—the lean-looking gluttonous cook, who eats most of what he cooks; the driver, who never finishes repairing the car; and the compounder, who for his undisturbed afternoon naps drives away the doctor's patients—appear mean and monstrous to little Ajayan. When the men spin yarns of ghosts to serve their own selfish ends, the lad's mind takes off on a flight of fright, fuelled by Grimm's fairy tales that Balu buys him. A life thus led, where the real, the unreal and the surreal merge, sows the seeds of Ajayan's mental imbalance.

Actually, it is more about mediocrity than madness, how mediocrity is not just tolerated, but glorified and worshipped to cover and protect the mass of patchiness. This is the community in which Ajayan grows up. The film is also about fantasy. His tendency—that progresses into a compulsive habit—to invent pushes him into a state where his mind cannot tell a lie from truth. When the servants talk about the *yakshi* or the female seductress, Ajayan naively believes them. These are indicators of what is to come. And, Ajayan finally sinks into a whirlpool.

Anantaram probes the duality of life, of the human mind.

Adoor says there is a constant conflict between the extrovert in us and the introvert. In some, one gets to be more dominating than the other. There is also a continuous tussle between rationality and irrationality. 'So Ajayan is trying to explain and grapple with a situation in his irrational frame of mind through rationalization. Ajayan is brilliant and extrovert, but suppressed into a dull introvert by a mediocre society. It does not want him to excel. So he withdraws, but his mind remains alert and active. He internalizes many things as he withdraws, and his imagination becomes more prolific. This is how the first part ends,' says Adoor on *Anantaram*.

'The second deals with the child/boy Ajayan, who was not allowed to differentiate between fact and fiction. He grows up in the midst of the three men who are mysterious. They behave strangely, feed him with lies. One man draws water from the well in blinding rain, but denies it is pouring. Another man says what they are drinking is not arrack, but medicine for their woes. When Ajayan says he too has his woes and would like some medicine, they laugh it off. They insist that a small boy cannot have woes,' Adoor says.

Finally, Suma comes into his life, a sister-in-law, who begins to appear less and less of a sister-in-law. Balu is like a brother to him, though not quite a brother. His foster father is like a parent, though not real enough. The ambivalence becomes total when Suma becomes Nalini.

Anantaram grew out of a real-life incident that Gopalakrishnan's wife, Sunanda, narrated a long time before the movie was conceived and made. In a hospital, a doctor adopted a new-born baby that had been abandoned by its mother. The woman could not be traced. The story bothered the auteur. He kept wondering what could have happened to the child: how did it grow up, how did it live, how did the doctor's family treat it and so on.

Often Gopalakrishnan's film ideas emerge from what he sees around him and what he hears. One of the questions that is invariably thrown at him is where does he get his ideas from. He has pondered over it, searched within himself. Finally, the answer hit him. The inspiration comes from life—what one has been living through; one's observations; from people and places; from newspapers and books; and from society at large. From anything and everything.

The next question is more difficult. Why is it that only some people get ideas? He feels that some are more sensitive and impressionable than others. 'Creativity defies simple definitions and explanations,' Adoor wrote in a book titled *A Door to Adoor*. 'It is common knowledge that a person without the faculty of memory is incapable of imagination and creativity. Memory is linked to experience. It is stored in images or ideas by combining previous experiences. Imagination is often regarded as the more seriously and deeply creative faculty, which perceives the basic resemblances between things, as distinguished from fancy—the lighter and more decorative faculty, which just takes in superficial resemblances.'

He further writes,

Experience is anything observed or lived through. It has many shades and grades. The most important is the individual reaction to things and events where one is directly involved.

At another level, experience is borrowed through empathy. You make the other person's experience your own in order to understand him and his predicament.

A different shade of experience is the one that comes from the appreciation of arts, literature, theatre, cinema, etc. . . . then, there is also the case of information as experience. Print and electronic media do provide daily information of life lived around us and elsewhere . . .

'These,' he tells me, 'are what enrich one's life. It is only such experiences that help a director make a movie that touches the heart and soul of an audience.'

Each of his films is personal and intimate, and leaves us with a sense of glowing satisfaction. His characters are varied and alive. Viswanathan is wracked by the guilt of not being able to keep Sita in comfort in *Swayamvaram*. Sankarankutty is reluctant to grow up in *Kodiyettam*. Sreedharan rises and then suffers the fall in *Mukhamukham*. And Ajayan challenges reality in *Anantaram*.

Did Gopalakrishnan feel for Ajayan, and how did he think of making him a schizophrenic? 'I have known a couple of people afflicted by the disease,' Adoor answers. I should have guessed that. He goes on, 'They have been very bright. I have also seen doctors beginning to behave like the patients they are treating. It is a slow mimetic change.'

Not only does his cinema seek motivation from real people and incidents but also takes place in life-like situations. He scouted around a lot to find Ajayan's house. Gopalakrishnan looked for a bungalow in the middle of a courtyard full of trees. He found one near Kottayam. The hospital where the doctor worked was the one run by the Tatas in Munnar. He is supposed to have worked in a hill resort, and the movie captures the rain and the mist of the mountains. Actually, the film was shot in many locations: on the Kovalam beach, in a house near Kollam and at the bus stop outside the University of Kerala (the erstwhile Travancore University) in Thiruvananthapuram.

The search for genuineness did not end with house hunting and location scouting. The ramshackle car, a Maurice Minor 8—under which the driver is to be found forever—was a new, gleaming contraption when it was handed over to Sivan for a few days' shoot. The car was ripped apart or almost and a coat of dust sprayed on it to make it look unused for a decade or two. The owner cried in shock and anger when he saw his car in such a terrible shape. But within two weeks of wrap-up, Sivan did a fine job on the car, and it looked much better than before.

The use of authentic locations and the right choice of actors help Gopalakrishnan achieve an amazing degree of believability. He then goes on to spin his reels, reflecting and analysing social conditions and mores. What is more, as the renowned director Shyam Benegal says in his foreword to *A Door to Adoor*, his movies 'are meditations on the human condition. He has an extraordinary ability to delve into the complexities of human existence; compulsions forced by history and tradition, and by the dynamics of social and political change.' Adoor's narratives appear simple at first, but as they unfold, nothing is simple any more. Protagonists are caught in moral ambiguities, and they are driven by social, environmental and historical factors.

Benegal describes him as 'probably the best director in India today'. Yet, more people know Satyajit Ray than they do Gopalakrishnan. Much more has been written about Ray than about Gopalakrishnan. All of Ray's films are available on disc, and hence many more people have watched them. Only two of Gopalakrishnan's works (*Nizhalkkuthu* and, more recently, *Elippathayam*) have been commercially released on disc.

Gopalakrishnan once took Bryan Walsh of *Time* to Chitranjali Studio to watch *Kathapurushan*. But they found that the first print of it had disintegrated in the tropical heat. Walsh writes: 'Adoor shakes his head and laughs gently. "When you see the print degrade like that, you realize what you do is ephemeral," he says. 'It's something you spend so much effort on, but it dissolves so quickly ... It need not.' Adoor says he has understood that and is trying to get all his work preserved on disc.

Meanwhile, his work is also being pirated: for instance, at Chennai's Burma Bazaar, which once hawked a variety of goods smuggled through the city's seaport. It still does, but not many go there, because import duties have been drastically cut and imports themselves are liberally allowed.

But the bazaar still thrives—on piracy, offering world cinema on quality CDs or DVDs at a tenth of the price of the original. Price apart, often an original Kiarostami or a Kurosawa or a Truffaut or a Ray or an Adoor Gopalakrishnan is not available at all, despite a growing tribe of Indians craving for a cinema that is different from the Bollywood-style song-and-dance formula. It is here that the cinema of India's one of living auteurs, Adoor Gopalakrishnan, assumes enormous significance.

If his 2002 *Nizhalkkuthu* (Shadow Kill), a disturbing story of a 1940s guilt-ridden hangman in Kerala, released on DVD by the Global Film Initiative in the US, is also to be found in its pirated version at Burma Bazaar, the message is not to be missed. The movies of the kind Adoor makes are beginning to create an impact in a country that churns out a thousand-odd films a year, a number that is twice as large as Hollywood's.

ANANTARAM

Cast and Credits

Year of production: 1987

Colour

Language: Malayalam

Duration: 125 minutes

Story, Screenplay and Direction: Adoor Gopalakrishnan

Chief Assistant: Meera Sahib

Producer: Ravi, General Pictures

Cinematography: Mankada Ravi Varma

Music: M.B. Srinivasan

Sound: Devadas, Krishnanunni and N. Harikumar

Art Direction: Sivan

Editing: M. Mani

Cast: Ashokan (Ajayan Senior), Sudheesh (Ajayan Junior), Mammootty (Balu), Shobana (Suma/Nalini), N.B. Thampi (doctor, Ajayan's foster father), Kaviyoor Ponnamma (Mother at the ashram)

Prizes: National Awards for Best Direction, Best Screenplay and Best Audiography; Kerala State Award for Best Direction; FIPRESCI (International Critics) Prize for the Best Film at the Karlovy Vary Film Festival in 1988

Festivals: Venice, Pesaro, Karlovy Vary, La Rochelle, Nantes, Amiens, Riga, Munich, Fribourge, Ljubljana, Helsinki, London, Washington DC, New York, San Francisco, Toronto, Hawaii and Alexandria among others

18

The Walls

In a way, *Mathilukal* (The Walls) was an extension of *Anantaram*. If the earlier film was about a creative process, *Mathilukal* focuses on literary inventiveness. Again, schizophrenia is a common feature: there is a subtle suggestion that *Mathilukal*'s protagonist, the renowned Malayalam writer Vaikom Muhammad Basheer, suffers from occasional bouts of the disorder.

For the first time, Gopalakrishnan chose someone else's story to make a movie. *Mathilukal* was an autobiographical novella, narrating Basheer's days in jail a few years before India's independence.

Adoor says this was not a story he happened to chance upon. It grew on him. Basheer has always been a part of him, and he has always admired the writer's perceptions, sense of humour and spirit of humanism. Gopalakrishnan read *Mathilukal* soon after it was published in 1967 in the annual issue of the Malayalam weekly, *Kaumudi*. Written in the first person, it chronicles Basheer's prison term in Thiruvananthapuram in 1942, five years before the British quit India.

In jail, he finds great company in a group of political detainees. He discovers some more through the delightful characters who take shape on his blank pages. He gets deeply involved with them as he does with fellow prisoners. Finally, when they are released and loneliness begins to gnaw at him, he falls in love with a woman prisoner, Narayani, on the other side of the jail wall. They never meet, but her voice and smell lift him from the shadow of solitude.

The woman could have been Basheer's figment of imagination. For, his proclivity for creation is well established. 'At first, she seems to be the projection of a lonely man, pining for a woman,' comments Suranjan Ganguly in *A Door to Adoor*. 'But gradually she comes to embody other concerns that are universal.' They talk to each other, and Narayani becomes central to his existence, so much so that when he is freed, he is disappointed and reluctant to go out, wondering what freedom is all about. Is it losing love? Basheer said the woman actually existed and they went through this bitter-sweet romance. At least, he believed so. Therein lies a certain ambiguity.

The film makes use of this vagueness to probe man's inner self in varying situations and conditions. If in *Anantaram*, Ajayan's schizophrenic state is analysed, in *Mathilukal* Basheer's physical displacement from his normal environment forms the basis of study. Ajayan's psychological dislocation forces him into a world where it becomes hard for him to differentiate between fact and fantasy. Basheer's incarceration takes him away from the familiar, and in the unfamiliar terrain, he is restless, sleepless and, maybe, schizophrenic. He has written about his illness, and says the medicines Ayurvedic doctors gave him made him drowsy, and were perhaps potent enough to put ten elephants to sleep.

In most cases, Adoor deals with the individual and his state of mind, and through the individual he makes a much wider statement on society. Here, it is Basheer.

Basheer (played in the movie by the Malayalam superstar Mammootty) embodies a free spirit, a free mind—reflecting the dream and desire of millions of Indians at that point in time. Basheer is a celebrated writer, whose prose mirrors the undying wish of the people to see a free India. Their longing translates into a cry and call for independence. Basheer embodies all this and at a time when Gandhi's Quit India Movement was at its strongest.

The work opens with Basheer languishing behind bars. He had been there for over a year without trial, his crime being *rajadroham* or treason against the state through his writings. His literary genius endears him to the most hardened of criminals as well as the toughest policemen. One police inspector is an admirer and supplies him with paper and writing material, despite wartime shortages—an act that can be considered seditious. He advises Basheer to go on hunger strike to provoke the authorities into producing him before a magistrate. Basheer is found guilty on many charges, mostly fabricated, and he is sentenced to two-and-a-half years of rigorous imprisonment.

At Thiruvananthapuram's Central Jail, he befriends policemen and prisoners, who are charmed by his wit and words. Basheer becomes privileged, and from beedis to biryani, from tea with sugar to the meatiest of fish are all there for the asking. The chief warder and the jailer grow fond of him.

He leads a comfortable life, and his joy and buoyancy are reflected in his relationships with just about everybody there—convicted murderers, other inmates and guards. Gopalakrishnan depicts a 'cosy atmosphere' within the four walls, and this was in keeping with the prevailing mood then. There was a growing expectation that the British—bled by World War II and with hundreds of thousands of their men killed and their material depleted despite their shameless colonial plundering—were tired of ruling faraway lands and desperate to march out of India. They were merely looking for a face-saving opportunity. The jail authorities felt that Basheer and the other political prisoners might well become the country's rulers. So, the prisoners were treated with a lot of respect and cordiality. Since the State of Travancore, where Thiruvananthapuram lay, was never directly under the British, the local administration was even more liberal and genial.

When the political prisoners leave—Basheer's name is strangely missing from the list of those to be released—he is lonely and even hatches a plot to escape. But suddenly the voice of a woman prisoner that wafts across the high wall, separating the men's wing from the women's, lifts his sagging spirit.

She is Narayani, the youngest there, the most beautiful, as she claims in the beginning. She has committed murder. But that does not stop Basheer from growing fond of her. Gopalakrishnan uses sheer eroticism to describe their meetings. There is tenderness, there is love and there is also the comic, but all kept at more than an arm's length by cold concrete. When Narayani tells Basheer that she is there next to the wall, he gently caresses it, his yearning for an affectionate touch perhaps shared by her as well. We are never taken to the other side. We never see Narayani. We only hear her. This posed challenges.

V. Abdullah, who translated all of Basheer's works into English, asked Gopalakrishnan how he planned to picture the scene where the protagonist smells the scent of the woman. Adoor replied that he would not even attempt it. Though it was a key point in the text, it would be repulsive to show Mammootty sniffing the air to catch Narayani's odour. Abdullah agreed.

Mathilukal posed many more challenges for Gopalakrishnan. For instance, how do you have a character without showing her at all? We only hear her voice. Adoor took a bold step when he decided that the film would never show Narayani.

Sixty voices were auditioned. The choice was between using an excellent but known voice and a not-so-good unknown voice. Eventually, Gopalakrishnan chose Lalitha, whose diction and intonation were flawless, but just about everybody in Kerala was familiar with her voice!

So what is wrong with this, one may ask. Narayani was a mysterious woman, or that is how she projects herself to Basheer, and that is how Basheer himself penned her character. But Lalitha's voice was so distinguished that it was a dead giveaway. The element of surprise is gone the moment we hear Lalitha! However, this is specific to only those familiar with Malayalam cinema and Lalitha.

There were many others who wanted to make this movie, and one even planned to cast six or seven attractive heroines, each playing the woman Basheer would have imagined every time he talked to her across the wall. This would have been totally at variance with Basheer's unique and original concept: a character who is heard and not seen.

The author agreed, gave the rights of his novella to Gopalakrishnan and offered him and his family small coins as a gesture of goodwill and appreciation. T. Ravindranathan Nair of General Pictures had had the film rights of the story for a decade, but he readily allowed Gopalakrishnan to obtain the rights from Basheer. Nair had by then produced three of Gopalakrishnan's movies. *Mathilukal* was sponsored by Doordarshan, India's Government-controlled television network, and produced by Adoor. This was the first venture of Adoor Gopalakrishnan Productions.

Mathilukal was certified by the censors on 31 December 1989, and premiered at the International Film Festival of India, held the following January in Kolkata. (The festival used to move around the country, going back to New Delhi every other year till 2004, when Panaji in Goa was chosen as the permanent venue. The festival thus threw away its gypsy cloak.)

Adoor says when the idea of filming *Mathilukal* struck him in the closing years of the 1980s, he found the story, which he first read in the late 1960s, still stimulating. He read most of

Basheer before he began scripting *Mathilukal*, and he saw a wonderful opportunity to traverse the writer's mind. There was also scope to recreate the man behind the words.

Though Basheer was absolutely fine with the idea of Gopalakrishnan making the movie, he still wanted to look at the script. He made this request as the two parted after the agreement had been sealed. Gopalakrishnan had merely smiled in reply. Obviously, he did not want to show the script, and be asked to make changes.

Nonetheless, when the film was ready, Gopalakrishnan made it a point to screen it first for Basheer, at Kozhikode, where he was living. He liked it immensely, and commented, 'Not a dull moment.' In fact, he particularly liked the way *Mathilukal* ended. In the novella, we see Basheer standing outside the jail gate with a rose in hand. He had been freed, and is probably waiting to meet Narayani still in prison. Narayani loves roses. The movie ends differently with Narayani throwing a dry branch in the air. It rises and falls against a vast blue sky. Basheer stands outside his cell, his eyes welling up, the tears blurring his vision of the branch in the air.

In a *Cinemaya* interview in 1994, Adoor said, 'When you adapt a story, it is very important that the film director sifts out the original and extracts a text which is all his own to follow. For instance, in the story there is a sentence, "I have kept watch over death." This single sentence has become a long sequence, quite central to the movie, beginning with the head warder waking up Basheer long before daybreak (and asking him to make tea). The convict to be hanged just before daybreak had asked for the drink. The viewer is around Basheer until the last bell rings for the convict. The whole scene is built up through little movements, exchanges of looks, dialogues in monosyllables, to get the viewer involved.'

In another departure from Basheer's prose, Gopalakrishnan builds up the sequences in such a way that we, the audience, begin to feel that Narayani is a figment of the author's imagination. Narayani did not really exist, though Basheer is emphatic that she does. In the first part of the picture, Basheer is unable to write, even though he wants to. In the second part, when he is lonely, after his political friends have left the prison, he begins to write. Probably, Narayani was a mere word on his pages. This is quite plausible. When Basheer could talk to a squirrel, talk to a bird and even to a tree, he could very well have invented a woman for company.

Soon after the first screening at Kozhikode, a young writer walked up to Gopalakrishnan and said he had not enjoyed watching the film as much as he did reading the novella. Gopalakrishnan explained to him that his work was not a literal translation of *Mathilukal*, and that it was an interpretation independent of the original The writer was not seemingly convinced. A little later, at a press conference, Basheer, who was also present, supported his director, turning, as Adoor put it, 'all the arrows into flowers and showering them all over the hall'. Caustic and humorous at the same time, Basheer was at his best. He then offered all his literary works to Adoor for adaptation without a fee.

Initially, Adoor says he had toyed with the idea of making Basheer's *Entuppuppakkoranendarnnu* (My Grandpa Had an Elephant), but it was too literary to transform it into visuals, and would not have done justice to the writer. Also, the kind of innocence he was referring to in it no longer existed. 'See, I am very particular that when I make a movie its appeal remains long after it has been made. Secondly, it must be true to the period. It must forge a relationship with time. Historically, it must be accurate. I may be telling a story, but it is only an excuse to sustain a viewer's interest in the life and times of the era my film is set in. Only then will the experience become richer for the viewer. He is not in the cinema merely to see a story unfold. He wants to see and feel the drama beneath the story. This is I why I dropped *My Grandpa Had an Elephant*.'

Mathilukal may have happened in 1942 at the height of the

Quit India movement, but it has a certain timelessness about it. Though Basheer wrote and published it in 1967 drawing upon his days of incarceration in 1942, the 1989 film version did not suffer because of the time lag. It works even today, because it basically addresses the idea of freedom.

Basheer wrote *Mathilukal* in the first person, but Gopalakrishnan recreated the writer as a character in a way that the two merged. Basheer evolved through his writings, and 'I had to shape him like that,' explains Adoor. The 1942 Basheer was not the literary giant he became later. Yet, the young man enjoyed some fame and recognition even then. To mould him into a figure like this, Gopalakrishnan borrowed characters and situations from some of Basheer's short stories, and incorporated them into the script of *Mathilukal*. An example of this is Razak (Ravi Vallathol), a murder convict who serves food to Basheer. 'I borrowed Razak from another story of Basheer's,' says Adoor. In *Mathilukal*, Razak kills his brother-in-law when he decides to divorce his wife, Razak's sister.

Some other characters emerged while Gopalakrishnan visited jails during his location scout. There are three central jails in Kerala: Thiruvananthapuram, Thrissur and Kannur. 'I went to all these places and talked to warders, jailers, superintendents and even under-trials. One or two characters emerged from my observations. And I found that the most well-behaved people in the jails were those convicted of murder. The worst were habitual housebreakers, and they were merciless. They even raped, and were unrepentant and beyond reform.'

Basheer himself was an insightful writer, his writings enriched by his compulsive travelling that took him all over India and even to Afghanistan. He was a keen chronicler, and his prose revealed that. He led a frugal life, living like a sage, sleeping in temples and mosques. Apart from his passion for writing and travelling, Sufism moved him: the rose plants that he tended so lovingly in the prison were a telling symbol of this faith. There is a scene in *Mathilukal* where Narayani asks him for a rose plant, and he digs out one and throws it to her across the wall.

In many ways, the movie is the most sensuous in the Adoor oeuvre. When it was screened at Rotterdam, a Chilean woman director said that she had never seen such an erotic man-woman union as the one in *Mathilukal*.

It also feels and looks authentic. Gopalakrishnan filmed *Mathilukal* in real locations or asked his art director Sivan to create one that was as real. The movie was shot in Thiruvananthapuram's Central Jail and in an actual police lockup in Haripad. The prison wall had to be repainted because the British used a special red-brick colour for their administrative buildings. Even in the 1980s, many Kolkata police stations sported this colour. Public buildings, such as the Connemara Library in Chennai, too were painted red.

Since shooting was not allowed inside the Central Jail after five in the evening, Gopalakrishnan asked Sivan to clone it in Chitranjali Studio. The wall, twenty-two feet high and 100 feet long, was built and embellished with moss and weeds. Unfortunately, it collapsed twice after a heavy rain, and had to be rebuilt. To add to this, the auteur contracted German measles. Yet he remained undaunted, pursuing perfection through intricate detailing.

Two sources helped achieve this: An eighty-year-old jail warder, who had retired as Inspector General of Police, and an old book, *The Administration and Governance of Jails and Police Stations*, that Meera Sahib found. With the help of these, Gopalakrishnan recreated the period piece complete with the clothes that people, prisoners and policemen wore then. The red-capped prisoners were convicted of murder, the black caps of lesser crimes. The whites were political detainees. Sivan designed all these to the last stitch and button. A very elaborate study went into getting right the costumes, the locales, the mood and the ambience.

Finally, Gopalakrishnan's choice of Mammootty was not without a good reason. The actor had already worked with the director in *Anantaram*. What is more, Mammootty was a great admirer of Basheer, had read him and knew him well. To play someone when he is living is no mean challenge, and the Malayalam star rose up to it.

So did the squirrels, though after throwing tantrum after tantrum. It took much coaxing, much cajoling and many takes before the squirrels put their tails up to perform. But by the time the principal shoot was over, a great amity between the men and the rodents had been established. Sadly, this had a flip side to it. These squirrels found themselves ostracized by the others in their own community who refused to accept them after they had been freed from prison! Unaccepted and isolated, the *Mathilukal* squirrels faced hostility and death from crows that seemed to have taken a cue or two from Hitchcock's *Birds*, though they attacked rodents not humans.

MATHILUKAL

Cast and Credits

Year of production: 1989

Colour

Language: Malayalam

Duration: 117 minutes

Story: Vaikom Muhammad Basheer

Screenplay and Direction: Adoor Gopalakrishnan

Chief Assistant: Meera Sahib

Producer: Adoor Gopalakrishnan Productions

Sponsor: Doordarshan

Cinematography: Mankada Ravi Varma

Music: Vijaya Bhaskar

Sound: N. Harikumar

Art Direction: Sivan

Costumes: Sivan

Editing: M. Mani

Cast: Mammootty (Basheer), Ravi Vallathol (Razak), Thilakan (head warder), Karamana Janardhanan Nair (political leader), P.C. Soman (head constable), Lalitha (Narayani's voice)

Prizes: National Awards for Best Direction, Best Actor (Mammootty), Best Audiography and Best Malayalam Film; FIPRESCI (International Critics) Prize at Venice, 1990 UNICEF Film Prize at Venice, 1990; Ecumenical Prize at Amiens; Awards for Best Film and Best Direction at the 2003 Auberville Film Festival for Youth

Festivals: Venice, Pesaro, Milan, Nantes, Manosque, Amiens, Munich, Fribourg, Rotterdam, Vienna, London, Ljubljana, Toronto, Los Angeles, Washington, New York, Hawaii, Istanbul and Haifa among others

19

The Servile

Every director has his favourites. Ray's mascot was Soumitra Chatterjee, an actor whose brilliance emanated from the auteur's megaphone. Ray first used him in *Apur Sansar* (The World of Apu), in 1959. This was followed by other films. There came a time when he immensely enriched the master's cinema.

Gopalakrishnan has had his favourites too, but the favouritism, if I may use this term for want of a better one, was evenly distributed. He used several actors several times. Karamana Janardhanan Nair, P.C. Soman, Vembayam Thambi, Somasekharan Nair, Thikkurissi Sukumaran Nair and Lalitha have been his regulars. If someone were to ask me who his most favourite was, I would look beyond these performers. It was his cinematographer, Mankada Ravi Varma. He worked on all his pictures except the last two, *Naalu Pennungal* and *Oru Pennum Randaanum*.

Ray seldom used stars, and when he did so on a few occasions, it was after considerable thought. When he cast Bengali matinee idol Uttam Kumar in *Nayak* (The Hero) in

1966, it was on the belief that none other than a star could do justice to the role of a star. *Nayak* was all about a star. Yet, Ray faced flak for using Uttam Kumar: Mrinal Sen quipped that Ray had now sunk to the level of using a matinee idol!

Gopalakrishnan had no such criticism coming his way when he had stars playing for him. Sarada was one, and a popular one at that, when he used her in *Swayamvaram* and *Elippathayam*. Madhu too was one when he did *Swayamvaram*. Later, Gopalakrishnan cast Malayalam matinee idol Mammootty in three consecutive movies beginning with *Anantaram*.

Mammootty's performances were riveting—certainly as Basheer and Bhaskara Patelar in *Vidheyan* (The Servile). Enacting Patelar after playing Basheer, Mammootty was marvellous the way he switched from a gentle, literary romantic—a charismatic soul loved by all in *Mathilukal*—to a brute, hated and despised by everybody in *Vidheyan*. Here men gravitated towards him out of fear and the power he exerted over them, reducing them to sheer servility. Spitting on and kicking the community's underdogs, Mammootty's Patelar is all viciousness. He kills, he rapes and strangles to death his lovely wife, Saroja (Tanvi Azmi), when she refuses to fall in line with his fearful ways.

The story is set in the early years of the 1960s when Thommi (M.R. Gopakumar) and his wife Omana (Sabita Anand) arrive in south Karnataka like hundreds of other Christian farmers who, forced by food shortages and unemployment in their native state of Kerala, migrated to neighbouring areas in search of better fortunes. Thommi and Omana are the last to arrive in an exodus that began during World War II, when rumours of large tracts of virgin land in Karnataka lured the Travancore (which became part of Kerala in 1956) peasants.

Thommi attracts the attention of Bhaskara Patelar, one among the Patels appointed by the British to collect taxes and enforce the law. Though the British left India in 1947, this system of revenue administration by Patels in vogue till the early 1960s, when Indian government officials took over. When Thommi and his wife arrive, Bhaskara has no legal powers, but he continues to bully the people around him through force and a handful of henchmen. Patelar terrorizes Thommi turning him into a meek mute, and rapes his wife. The rape turns into an open affair with Patelar being both a depriver and a provider for the couple.

Things come to a head when Patelar is tailed by Saroja's relatives after he murders her and his attempt to camouflage his crime as suicide fails. Hunted and chased into the wilderness by a couple of hired gunmen, Patelar is finally shot dead.

This is probably the only nail-biting finish in the Adoor basket. As the gunmen pursue Patelar into a rocky forest and corner him—half naked, hungry, hurt and shamed, his arrogance humbled and his might destroyed—Thommi, who flees along with his master, hides behind a huge boulder. The gunshots rent the air, and we see Patelar with his gun-toting arms raised slump on the rocky floor in a pool of blood. For a full minute, Thommi does not know what to do. How should he react? Should he be happy and relieved now that Patelar's cruel dominance has ended or should he mourn the loss of one who was also his provider? Thommi makes his way to Patelar, removes the gun from him, throws it into the gushing stream nearby and takes to his heels calling out to Omana at the top of his voice, 'The master is dead, the master is dead.'

Vidheyan, based on a Paul Zacharia work (*Bhaskara Patelarum Ente Jeevithavum* [Bhaskara Patelar and My Life], 1986), was the second adaptation by Gopalakrishnan. It is a deep analysis of servility in the wider context where the servant-master relationship takes on a strange hue. After the initial anger, pain and reluctance, Thommi finds pleasure in this slavery and obedience to the extent that he even finds his wife's sexual affair with Patelar exciting. In bed one night with his wife, Thommi says he likes the way she smells, Patelar's expensive perfume having rubbed off on her. Such is the vicarious joy.

It is only in the end when Patelar and Thommi are fugitives in the picturesque forest that they become equals, dressed alike and eating the same food—and from the same leaf. This is the end of the sadistic bondage that Thommi had been in, and when he finds himself free he is confused. He does not know how to face it or cherish it.

Vidheyan is a far more ambitious effort than Gopalakrishnan's earlier films and probes into the psyche of the society rather than the individual. Patelar and Thommi at the two extreme ends of a wide spectrum help in this study. One represents absolute authority and the other absolute servility, both monstrous and distasteful in vastly different ways. Patelar is not after wealth here. That is not how he hopes to gain and retain power. He seeks it through the spread of terror, through violence, liberally using his foot to kick hapless men.

This is how he builds a power base hoping to replace one that disappeared after legislation empowered government officials to take charge of revenue and administrative matters. Patelar fantasizes about authority and uses physical force to violate women like Omana and terrorize men like Thommi.

In many ways, the story is macabre and nudges you to reflect on evil. Adoor says the original narrative was far more violent and he excised some parts and toned down others. A lot is left unsaid in the classic Gopalakrishnan style: the opening titles play over an armless chair against which a rifle leans. The chair placed outside a toddy shop acts as a harbinger of things to come. While the gun denotes power, the broken chair denotes decadent feudalism, whose last signs are ebbing out.

Adoor tells me that though this movie is different from what he did till then, there is a thread of continuity running across his entire cinema. Spirituality is one, though it is never overt.

The first time Thommi gets up and walks across the street to meet Patelar, the church bell rings far away. Christians will recognize it as the funeral toll. At the end, when Thommi is running back home, the church bell sounds again, but this time it is for congregation. Between these two gongs, we see a parish priest asking Thommi why he does not come for confession. There is another striking sequence that suggests spirituality: Patelar wants to dynamite the sacred fish in the village pond, despite Thommi's plea against such a sinful act. Well, the device fails to explode, and the tiny creatures swim on.

All these imply that Thommi is not really a sinner. He is forced into sin by fear and depravation, and in a scene illustrative of this, we see him beg of Patelar not to kill his wife. In a way, Patelar himself is a victim of circumstance and background: after he strangles Saroja, he is gripped by guilt, and seeks constant reassurance from Thommi that she could not have known who her murderer was. Unfortunately, Patelar does not heed Providence. His first attempt to kill Saroja misfires, and he could have easily stopped himself there and tried reforming. Instead, he tries again and succeeds, a success that drives him towards the frightening finale.

In the end, in a strange twist of images, Patelar begins to look and behave like Thommi. A quirk of fate pushes one to doom and the other to possible freedom and salvation. But is it? It is likely that a character such as Thommi will be happy and content only in slavery, and he might as well seek out another tyrant to take charge of his life.

In *A Door to Adoor*, Gopalakrishnan says, 'The possibility cannot be ruled out. Yes, even the freedom he gains at the end maybe for the time being. For someone who knows Thommi, his final run may not be one of liberation. He is not running out of joy. There is also an element of sadness in it. His cry also resembles a wail ... He is terribly attached to his possessions, whether it is his wife or land. Maybe it is this attachment that leads him to slavery.'

Unlike Basheer, Zacharia was not very pleased with the way Gopalakrishnan filmed the written work. Reams of newsprints have been used—call it wasted—on the Zacharia–Adoor disagreement.

Zacharia tells me that he took objection to the fact that the helmer told an interviewer that the book was merely a take-off point. 'I think Adoor followed my story completely,' he avers. But Adoor says he did make a few changes (as he did in *Mathilukal*): 'I gave Omana and Saroja greater importance than what they got in the book. Zacharia's Patelar kills his wife for property, but mine does not. There is only a single murder in my film, the murder of conscience (wife Saroja) by Patelar. Zacharia had made him into a serial killer. I did not want to do that.'

Gopalakrishnan's *Vidheyan* clearly portrays the softer side of Patelar; there are moments when we feel that he loves his wife and child deeply, and when he is alone without his cronies, he is contemplative, almost mellow. It is his sidemen who seem to empower him with malice.

In another scene, Gopalakrishnan draws on the Bible to prove that faith saves. While Zacharia's dynamite explodes in the fish pond, Gopalakrishnan's does not. 'I wanted to show that Thommi's belief—despite the fact that he is not a Hindu—prevails. He believes that the fish is protected by Hindu gods, and they in turn safeguard the village. When the dynamite fails, it indicates the triumph of faith,' Adoor adds.

Whatever may have been the misunderstanding between the writer and the director, I feel that if Zacharia were to have presumed that his text would remain unaltered in the hands of someone like Gopalakrishnan, given to free thinking and artistic independence, he could not have been more wrong.

At this point, a natural question would be, why did Adoor go for a second literary adaptation after *Mathilukal*. Adoor smiles, looks guilty, and explains: 'I became very lazy after

Mathilukal. Two or three years had passed and I began to feel that I had to make a movie. Somehow I could not hit upon an idea for a story. Then I thought of one written by Zacharia that was published in an annual issue of the Malayalam journal, *Mathrubhoomi*. This was also a novelette. Probably, even shorter, though longer than a short story.' Zacharia is supposed to have written it in a hurry, sending in a page at a time to the publisher.

Gopalakrishnan's script went beyond Zacharia's text: 'I had to place the story in the context of history. Travancore Christians were hard working and some of them prospered in the new land, Karnataka, that they made their home. Of course, some like Thommi had their share of unpleasantness. They faced tyrannical landlords, who were feudal in their outlook and tried imposing archaic laws. When my film opens, the government had already taken control of revenue and administration, though the earlier enforcers, the Patelars, still exerted considerable influence through a rein of terror and subjugation.'

Authority becomes oppressive when it is accepted without question. This can happen even in a democracy. It can be vicious even in a democratic set-up. Adoor opines that servility is ingrained in the Indian psyche, and this is one reason why we have not become a truly democratic state. And we have characters such as Bhaskara Patelar. He was born into this system and he thinks that he has a natural right over others' lives. And he wants to use it fully. But he could have been checked, if the others were not so implicitly obedient. There is no protest. No dissent.

Before principal photography, Gopalakrishnan and Zacharia visited the Karnataka–Kerala border, where the writer has a small estate, growing rubber and cashew. They visited many Patelar homes. Many of them live in poverty today, and have just about a shell for a house. The director finally chose Ramakrishna Rai's house, a typical Patelar dwelling. Some work had to be done there, including the furnishing.

Gopalakrishnan's search took him to Mangalore and Kasargode, where he spotted Patelar furniture, including the large bed on which Bhaskara sleeps and later strangles his wife.

The broken chair was more elusive. He went to St. Aloysius College in Mangalore with a Kannada professor friend, Dr Damodar Shetty, who said that an old, armless chair was part of the junk there. The two went to meet the Principal, a Christian priest, in his room. He was reading a file before him. Shetty told the Principal: 'Sir, he has come to look at old furniture.' The Principal looked up and asked Gopalakrishnan, 'Are you the carpenter?' Adoor replied, 'Sort of . . .' For, who else, the Father might have wondered, could have come looking for a broken chair! This piece of furniture finally landed on the set, and later on the frame. Even the movie's brochure displays the chair on the cover—the chair that symbolizes the decay of the Patelar raj as he stubbornly refuses to yield power. The armless wooden piece is a telling sign, a remarkable way of conveying a message forcefully.

Vidheyan was shot inside Karnataka, close to the Kerala border. Gopalakrishnan and his team chose a spot there and built a toddy shop and a few other shops. The place after Sivan's art endeavour resembled a street junction with a bus stop. When the set was complete and shooting was to begin, some Christian settlers who had their shops and houses there threatened to pull down their thatched roofs and replace them with tiles. This would have marred the period look of the place. Adoor's team pleaded with them not to do this until the shooting was over. The settlers demanded an unreasonably high sum of money to keep their thatches on. Finally, a compromise was reached after Meera Sahib and Zacharia went to the local Christian priest for help.

There was more drama to come. A rumour spread that there had been someone like Bhaskara Patelar around. The local Patelars had seemed annoyed that a film was being made on them. The rumour became wilder, when it was whispered that a rifle-toting Patelar would appear on the set. Well, the rumour turned out to be just that, a rumour, and no Patelar actually turned up. But Adoor says that a Patelar might have been part of the curious onlookers, keeping watch over the shoot!

It was one of his most difficult movies. The actual photography by itself was a Herculean task. The locations were often inside dense forests. Sometimes, there was no road at all there, and the heavy cinema equipment had to be lugged by men. The movie crew doubled up as coolies.

A full-length feature could have been made on the making of *Vidheyan*. When it was shot, it was summer, the scorching heat and the parched land causing immense discomfort. But Gopalakrishnan, his principal actors, the cameraman and other crew members were not to be daunted. They carried on.

The auteur's search for a waterfall was another adventure, though dangerous. Gopalakrishnan, Meera Sahib and Zacharia's manager, Chandran Pillai, began a treacherous journey through dense foliage and growth—walking downhill and clearing vegetation with the help of choppers. Little did they know then that there was a highly poisonous king cobra close to where they were. However, it was worth the effort, and they chanced upon the waterfall.

The following day, after the camera had been set up and the actors had taken up their positions, the sky suddenly turned menacingly dark. It began raining heavily, and someone in the group warned the others that there could be flash floods. The moment Mammootty heard this, he ran for his life, climbing up the hill to reach for the road, and safety. Dressed in just a dhoti, he cut and bruised himself in panic. Not a flattering image for a superstar whose heroic deeds on the screen leave many envious.

His reaction got the others nervous as well, and just about everybody was seen racing up the steep hillside towards the road. The day may have been thrilling, but it was frustrating for Gopalakrishnan. The schedule could not be completed, and, worse, carting the heavy equipment up and down the steep incline was no joke.

The film, however, turned out to be extraordinarily engaging. To begin with, Gopalakrishnan had a good plot to work on. Zacharia's story was a classic that the scriptwriter in Gopalakrishnan tackled by adding details and giving it a completely new interpretation. When one looks back and thinks about the movie, both Patelar and Thommi appear less disgraceful. They are in different ways hapless victims of situation.

The only thriller in the Adoor oeuvre, *Vidheyan* was mostly shot at night to give that eerie feeling of fright and evil. When the shoot was wrapped up, Adoor says he felt trapped and wanted to escape. It was a terrible feeling of being boxed in. And he had to get out into the sunshine and feel a sense of liberation. He did by walking into a story that was dear to him. For, it was his own. Or almost.

VIDHEYAN

Cast and Credits

Year of production: 1993

Colour

Languages: Malayalam and Kannada

Duration: 112 minutes

Story: Paul Zacharia

Screenplay and Direction: Adoor Gopalakrishnan

Chief Assistant: Meera Sahib

Producer: Ravi, General Pictures

Cinematography: Mankada Ravi Varma

Music: Vijaya Bhaskar

Sound: Devdas and T. Krishnanunni

Art Direction: Sivan

Costumes: Sivan

Editing: M. Mani

Cast: Mammootty (Bhaskara Patelar), M.R. Gopakumar (Thommi), Sabita Anand (Omana), Tanvi Azmi (Saroja)

Prizes: National Awards for Best Actor (Mammootty) and Best Regional Film; Kerala State Awards for Best Film, Best Director, Best Actor (Mammootty) and Best Story; FIPRESCI (International Critics) Prize at Singapore, 1994; Inter-film Prize, Manheim, 1994

Festivals: London, Pesaro, Nantes, Brussels, San Sebastian, Fribourg, Munich, Mannheim, Rotterdam Ljubljana, Singapore, Hong Kong, Fukuoka, Brisbane, Durban, Teheran, Toronto, New York, San Francisco, Chicago, Hawaii and Sao Paulo among others

20

The Man of the Story

Gopalakrishnan's films, mostly, have an autobiographical undertone. Sometimes, it is strong. At other times, it lurks beneath the story. *Kathapurushan*, released in 1995, was his own story in many ways. Adoor has said several times that cinema or, for that matter, a novel or short story is invariably based on or inspired by life's experiences. These can be very prominent in some cases. I think *Kathapurushan* (The Man of the Story) falls under this category. The 'Man' here is Gopalakrishnan himself. The 'Story' is his own. Or just about.

The movie was shot in the house his maternal grandfathers built at Pallickal in Adoor—the house where Gopalakrishnan was born and spent most of his childhood. His birth was difficult, like Kunjunni's (the film's protagonist played by Viswanathan). His parents are separated, like the helmer's, though Gopalakrishnan's father did occasionally visit his family. Kunjunni's never does. There was a Veluchar, estate manager (Babu Namboothiri plays this role in the movie), at Pallickal as well, though his name was different. The manager loved the boy Gopalakrishnan as dearly as he did his own family. But

Kathapurushan's Veluchar does not have a family, and Gopalakrishnan was one among several siblings, unlike Kunjunni, who is the only child. There is Meenakshi (actress Mini Nair), Kunjunni's childhood sweetheart whom he later marries.

I once asked Adoor, rather mischievously, if he'd been in love with anyone. Not in its real sense, he said, and his marriage with Sunanda was conventionally arranged. She grew up in Malaysia, can speak Malay, and was at one point of time not very comfortable with Malayalam. Later, I suppose, her husband helped her to get conversant with the language, its literature and culture.

The parts in the film that deal with Kunjunni's childhood and boyhood years have been drawn from the director's memories and life. But memory can play tricks. It can be selective. Adoor remembers a blind man who used to visit his home telling him and others delightful stories. He would also act them out. Years later, when Gopalakrishnan asked his brothers and sisters about the blind man, only one remembered him. That is memory. It is an interesting phenomenon. It is a question of what affects you, what moves you and what does not. I suppose some experiences refuse to go away, staying all along with you till they become an integral part of you.

There were some landmark events that Gopalakrishnan witnessed and was so touched that he still remembers them. These events he lets Kunjunni see as well. India's independence, Gandhi's assassination, Communist rule in Kerala, land reforms, Naxalite movement and the black Emergency under Indira Gandhi are some events that the auteur and his hero live through. 'It was an emotional journey for me,' Adoor says.

Kunjunni grows up in a home where his parents are separated. Though his mother (Urmila Unni), ailing most of the time (somewhat like Gopalakrishnan's), and his maternal grandmother, Muthassi (Arnamula Ponnamma), shower him with love and care, the boy misses his father. In a way,

Veluchar fills this vacuum. The maidservant, Janamma's (played by Lalitha) daughter, Meenakshi, adores Kunjunni and is fiercely protective of him.

At college, Kunjunni—like many sensitive young men of the time and perhaps influenced by his uncle, Vasu (Narendra Prasad), who gives up Gandhism for Marxism—begins to follow the Communist ideology. The death of his mother and the land reforms under the first elected Communist Government in Kerala that take away the family's agricultural plots profoundly affect Kunjunni's family. When the deprived family has to send away the maid and her daughters, including Meenakshi, he is shattered but helpless.

He begins to feel that revolution is the answer to the country's ills, and like hundreds of young men of that time, Kunjunni becomes a Naxalite and runs a printing press publishing inflammatory literature. The movement is crushed by the administration. Kunjunni is arrested and tortured, and left with a limp, a legacy of police brutality.

Finally, when the courts acquit him, he goes looking for Meenakshi. They marry and settle down, and when he sells his huge house and property, he finds his peace. The tag of *petty bourgeois* that his schoolteacher once ridiculed him with is gone forever.

Tracing metaphorically a period of forty-five years beginning with Kunjunni's birth around 1937, Gopalakrishnan weaves a compelling story of changing times. We see Kunjunni as a little boy who stutters and prefers to look at a goat from his classroom rather than chant the Malayalam alphabet along with the other students. When the teacher waves the stick and frightens him out of his distraction, forcing him to recite the lesson, Kunjunni stutters even more. The incident strongly hints that tradition is about to pass, and Veluchar is horrified. He holds the emerging Marxist ideas responsible for emboldening the teacher to walk past Kunjunni's house without respectfully removing his footwear. Ironically, it is Veluchar and his ilk who are themselves beneficiaries of this transformation.

The servants may keep their distance from the family, but there is some kind of egalitarianism in this relationship. Veluchar is almost part of the family. So too is Meenakshi, her siblings and her mother. If Meenakshi's father, the elephant-keeper Pachupillai (Oduvil Unnikrishnan), is not as welcome as the rest of his clan, it is only because of his philandering. 'The relationship between human beings was very intense. It went beyond the economic sphere. Servants were like members of the house. In Kerala, houses for cattle were as decorative as houses for humans, and even animals were part of the family,' Adoor told *The Times of India* interviewer in 1996.

In the end, when Kunjunni marries Meenakshi—despite her father's arrogant disinclination that emerges out of his drunken stupor and frustration rather than any indoctrination of Marxist values—it signals refreshing equality. Pachupillai asks Kunjunni to pay a bride price of Rs 10,000. Janamma is shocked, but he insists that Meenakshi is paying a much higher price by agreeing to live with a poor handicap like Kunjunni. He agrees at once, and cements the love he has had for her, and she for him. This is a touching sequence, as touching as an earlier one between the two on the banks of a pond.

Two incidents seal and strengthen this concept of equality. Veluchar, staunchly anti-Gandhi, disappears without a trace, and with him the last bastion of feudalism in Kunjunni's household. It is very clear that Veluchar believes in class distinctions. Secondly, his father's death cuts Kunjunni completely from the past and propels him towards a unique future. When he sells his house and land and moves into a smaller place, the shift may appear cosmetic but, nonetheless, it helps him break out of a decadent culture. Gopalakrishnan symbolically conveys this to us by showing a stutter-free Kunjunni at the end. His little son joyously tells his mother that his father no longer stutters, and the three begin to chant the alphabet that Kunjunni once found so hard to pronounce. A poignant way of drawing curtains over an era.

Adoor tells me that every system must adapt and change. It must keep in mind the needs of the time. Otherwise, it can spell disaster. Unni in *Elippathayam* and Bhaskara Patelar in *Vidheyan* owe their downfall to their mulishness. Unni is thrown into cold water, something he dreads all along, and the other pays with his life. Kunjunni is unlike either: he embraces change, even telling his deprived family that the land must rightfully belong to its tillers.

His life moves along the upward gradient of a graph, so to say. Political awareness grows and matures into a state when Kerala becomes the first place anywhere in the world to have a duly elected Communist government. It was the first state to introduce land reforms. This led to some aberrations, such as the birth of Naxalism and its notion of armed revolution. Adoor is candid enough to admit that he appreciates their ideology, but never their means to achieve it or put it into practice. 'I am a Gandhian. I can never support violence,' he looks grave.

But has he ever had Leftist leanings? Adoor does not answer this question directly. 'I feel disturbed when people are not given the opportunity to develop themselves. I feel very sad when I see somebody very talented having to stop his education because he has no financial support. These are inequalities which cannot be really glossed over or pardoned,' he rues.

Kathapurushan, in this regard, is a fascinating social document presented through fascinating visuals. Shots of Veluchar taking Kunjunni to school across lush green paddy fields, and Congressmen carrying black flags and walking in a single file to mourn Gandhi's death are images that remain etched in my memory. Some of the indoor scenes also look magnificent, the architecture breathing history.

Vibrant, optimistic, the movie portrays a picture of tranquillity in the first half. The boy's occasional distress at school and tiffs with a teasing Meenakshi are nothing compared to what he will face later. Maybe Adoor was telling us that serenity can often be deceptive, and peace is invariably the casualty of change. A new order can come in only through turmoil.

The tumult comes in various forms: Kunjunni's fatherless existence and the shock of seeing him dead, not alive, at the end, his own suffering in jail, the death of his mother and the degeneration of the political climate into extremism. Yet, Kunjunni remains steadfast in his convictions and upholds an honest way of living. There is one telling scene, where he gets handcuffed and goes back to prison after performing the last rites of his grandmother. On a short parole for the sombre ceremony, he does not waver despite being tempted and prodded by his friend to escape at a moment when the policemen guarding him at the crematorium are relaxed and looking the other way. His integrity reflects a beautiful innocence that we see in many of Gopalakrishnan's characters. Sankarankutty, Thommi and Basheer in particular are an epitome of virtue. This is typical of Gopalakrishnan, who usually paints it in all its disarming hues.

John W. Hood writes in *The Essential Mystery: Major Filmmakers of Indian Art Cinema* that the film's 'innocence is highlighted by keeping to the background the guile of politicians, the power of the police and the artifice of censorship'. Undoubtedly so. We are spared the details of police torture. Apart from a truncheon being thrust into Kunjunni, the rest of the third-degree methods are left to the viewer's imagination. The raid on the printing press is handled with admirable restraint.

There is, however, a point where Gopalakrishnan is severe: when Veluchar pleads with the police officer to let Kunjunni out so that he may have a last glimpse of his dying grandmother, the man in uniform jeers, 'Let her die, and then we shall see.' He is cruel. Veluchar is physically thrown out, and one cannot miss the picture of Gandhi on the wall. The director drives his point with subtlety.

As much as *Kathapurushan* may be a chronicle of the time and the community, it goes beyond this—as does the rest of Gopalakrishnan's cinema. This movie is an intensely personal story of courage. It does not, therefore, overburden one with too much of history. Otherwise it could have had the feel of a documentary. We do have history but only that much to help us understand the characters and the situations they find themselves in. Veluchar, for instance, would have looked flat and two-dimensional if the film had remained silent about the political developments of the day, developments that perhaps hastened the end of feudalism.

Adoor Gopalakrishnan is an artist with an exceptionally keen awareness of the intricate connections between the individual and greater social and historical forces, a man whose work reflects a ready sympathy for human frailty as much as with strength . . .' The unhurried pace of the narrative sets the atmosphere. There are two places in the movie that I would like to point out. One, when the Ayurvedic physician (P.C. Soman) is reading out his prescription for the mother. The list of medicines and dos and don'ts appears endless. Two, when she dies, the rituals go on for a long time. Adoor explains why he kept these two scenes long. 'Ayurveda is not a quick medicine. It does not offer you quick remedy. I paced it that way. The way he reads out is slow and deliberate. As far as the death of the mother is concerned, it is detailed. I show her ill, and when she dies the ritualistic practices are all presented. However, when the grandmother passes away, I show only the cremation. Finally, in the case of Kunjunni's father, not even this is seen. Kunjunni tells Meenakshi when he returns from his father's house that by the time he reached there everything was over.'

(Sivan has an interesting incident to narrate here. For the grandmother's cremation, they had used a lot of firewood, and after the shoot, when he was dismantling it he found a huge cobra that could have well bitten him when he was setting it all up!)

The film gets even subtler when Meenakshi's father tells Kunjunni's grandmother that since the elephant has been sold he has become a marriage broker. The old lady quips, 'So you are a *hamsam* [swan] these days.' This refers to *Nalacharitam*, where Prince Nala asks a swan to take his message of love to his beloved, Damayanti. Adoor says that with a single word so much can be conveyed. But for those not familiar with *Nalacharitam* (a part of the Mahabharata), the nuances may be lost.

The movie's lead characters, Viswanathan and Mini, had to be moulded into the characters they play. This was Viswanathan's second film with Gopalakrishnan after *Mukhamukham*. Adoor cast him for two reasons. He had a sensitive face and was the son of a family friend. It is a pity, though, that he no longer works in cinema, running a computer firm instead. The director had to work on him to get him into the character. But he had to work harder on Mini, who again was actually his find.

Love between the characters they play is a strong factor. In most of his movies, his protagonists are middle-aged men: Sankarankutty in *Kodiyettam* is well past the conventional age of marriage. Basheer in *Mathilukal* is in his forties. Unni in *Elippathayam* and Sreedharan in *Mukhamukham* are older men. It is only in *Anantaram* and *Kathapurushan* that the men are in their youth. So one finds their relationship with women warm and energetic, certainly in *Kathapurushan*, where the romance between Meenakshi and Kunjunni develops naturally. We see the young Meenakshi tease and trouble the boy Kunjunni, much to the chagrin of Veluchar, who is appalled that a servant's daughter could have the guts to play equal with the young master of the house. I wonder what would have happened had Veluchar been around when Meenakshi and Kunjunni marry: he might have thrown a fit.

In the final analysis, 'Gopalakrishnan,' as *Variety* said in 1996, 'keeps all the big events off screen. This could easily have been a sweeping epic along *Doctor Zhivago* lines, but instead remains firmly rooted in the minor events of the hero's life. The Naxalite uprising is portrayed only via newspaper headlines; Kunjunni's prison experiences aren't shown . . .'

But is this not how Gopalakrishnan wanted his Man of the Story to be?

KATHAPURUSHAN

Cast and Credits

Year of production: 1995

Colour

Language: Malayalam

Duration: 107 minutes

Story, Screenplay and Direction: Adoor Gopalakrishnan

Producers: Adoor Gopalakrishnan Productions and Japan Broadcasting Corporation (NHK)

Cinematography: Mankada Ravi Varma

Music: Vijaya Bhaskar

Sound: N. Harikumar

Art Direction: Sivan

Make-up: P.N. Mani

Editing: M. Mani

Cast: Viswanathan (Kunjunni), Mini Nair (Meenakshi), Arnamula Ponnamma (Kunjunni's grandmother Muthassi), Urmila Unni (Kunjunni's mother), Narendra Prasad (Vasu), Babu Namboothiri (Veluchar), Lalitha (Janamma), Oduvil Unnikrishnan (Pachupillai), P.C. Soman (Ayurvedic physician)

Prizes: National Awards for Best Film and Best Supporting Actress (Arnamula Ponnamma); FIPRESCI (International Critics) Prize at MAMI, Mumbai, 1997; Special Jury Award at Singapore, 1996

Festivals: Toronto, London, Nantes, Pesaro, Rotterdam, Goteborg, Ljubljana, Munich, Vienna, Fribourge, Washington DC, New York, Denver, Hawaii, Paris, Tokyo and Fukuoka among others

21

Shadow Kill

It seemed that *Kathapurushan* said just everything that needed to be. Gopalakrishnan had drawn inspiration largely from his own life to make this film. Years went by, and except for two well-researched and well-made documentaries—*Kalamandalam Gopi*, 1999, and *Koodiattam*, 2001—he made nothing. No feature, and there were thoughts that the helmer's career was fading out. Till *Nizhalkkuthu* (Shadow Kill) faded in. When it finally hit the screens in 2002, it was a good seven years after his last fiction feature.

Nizhalkkuthu, set in 1941 when Gandhi's freedom struggle was gathering momentum, turned out to be a work that dealt

---

Note: 'Shadow kill' has its origins in the Mahabharata. The Kauravas, desperate to kill their foster brothers, the Pandavas, realize that till Lord Krishna is with the Pandavas, they cannot die. The Kauravas then get a sorcerer to perform black magic, whereby images resembling the Pandavas are killed. As each image falls, the actual Pandava who resembles it dies as well. This is what is called killing a shadow, the shadow here being the image.

with a highly emotional and controversial subject—capital punishment. He treated it with the gentleness of a breeze, even listening to it and making it a character in his movie.

'When he's shooting a film, Adoor Gopalakrishnan doesn't listen to his actors, critics or the government nor does he pander to his audience. He does, however, listen to the wind while shooting his latest movie, *Shadow Kill*, the story of an anguished hangman in 1940s India. Adoor was struck by the nighttime gusts playing on palmyra leaves.

Adoor elaborates further: 'I was excited by the sound that mimicked the human heartbeat. I immediately knew that I had to catch the spirit of it and make it the heartbeat of the movie. In fact, the sound was the work of the gushing wind passing through the palmyra leaves. The palmyra tree was inviting itself to be a character, which it eventually became. So did the wind.'

Adoor goes on, 'I researched a lot about the life and times of the last executioner of the Travancore State. Story and history intertwine here.

'It was not easy to locate a place that had the right ambience and appearance. We had to find a locale that defied time to look as it existed sixty years ago—one with huge rock formations in the background and flowering palmyra trees all around. But Kanyakumari district, where Nagercoil lies, had changed completely. The region once known for its wealth of palmyra trees had by then become bare, with all signs of modernity visible just about everywhere. I was growing desperate. What I had in mind for the locale was nowhere to be seen. We had already combed the area in and around Nagercoil. After days of futile search, when my hope was beginning to fade, we reached Pottalkulam, in the foothills of the Maruthuva Malai (Medicinal Hill). The sun had already set. Soon, the hills and valley would be enveloped by darkness. And then it happened. Way down a narrow lane, there stood a small house which looked exactly like what I had in mind.

This house with alterations would become the hangman's home.

'The setting was perfect as a cluster of palmyra trees stood behind the house. The one, the tallest, was to witness the lives of the house's inmates, a family that lived just outside the village and in social isolation.'

For, the ruler of the pre-independence princely State of Travancore—of which Kanyakumari was a part—felt that such segregation would help the executioner and his family remain emotionally detached from the community. Perhaps, this also helped lessen the agony and anger the society may have harboured against him. Often considered a 'dealer in death', a hangman was feared, and perceived as devilish. Here was a man who killed another man in cold blood, even if it was on the explicit order and command of the state.

Strangely, the ruler himself was never the victim of his subjects' displeasure or rancour, because he had found a devious way of absolving himself of the guilt. Minutes before every execution, he would despatch a royal courier with an order pardoning the convict. However, the order would be so timed to reach the prison after the hanging was over! (Adoor avers that even the Spanish king did this till the late 1960s.) The man who would pull the rope would be left with deep remorse. And he would carry the cross of culpability.

The ruler of Travancore was required to project himself as a devout practising Hindu who regularly worshipped (the scions still do) at Thiruvananthapuram's Sree Padmanabha Swamy Temple. The state is formally dedicated to the deity of this temple and the ruler rules on behalf of the Lord. This is probably why the ruling family had to appear to dispense divine mercy and compassion. Albeit ritualistically.

Indeed, *Nizhalkkuthu* assumes enormous significance because of its stress on the guilt of an executioner. This is no ordinary tale of a hangman and his hangings. According to *Cahiers du Cinéma*, the respected French film journal (founded in 1951 by

André Bazin and others and whose distinguished writers included François Truffaut, Jean-Luc Godard, Jacques Rivette and Claude Chabrol), 'In a simple life story of an executioner of the forties who could no more withstand executing innocent people, the tragedy gets intrigued by an unexpected second part narration of a story within a story—a fiction that the character owns and develops by himself leading to his own peril.'

The movie opens with Kaliyappan (Oduvil Unnikrishnan) in a toddy shop telling others how he hanged on the ruler's order an innocent man. 'But that is what every man who stands facing the noose says,' someone in the shop tells Kaliyappan. 'No, no, but this man was truly innocent,' Kaliyappan is categorical even in his inebriated state. The mood is thus set for a moving narrative.

To alleviate his misery, the ruler takes good care of him. He is given farmlands and annual monetary benefits, and gifts after every execution. He is housed on the periphery of the village, so that he has little idea about the convict he is to execute or the preceding legal proceedings. (Even in ancient Switzerland, the hangman's house was outside his village, as Adoor found during his travels.) His job is to hang the guilty, not to question the judicial verdict. Not even sympathize with the condemned.

But *Nizhalkkuthu*'s Kaliyappan is quite different, from the popular perception of an executioner. He does not appear tall, hefty and fearsome. He looks small, meek and genteel, almost unbelievably so. Above all, he is extremely human and kind. And sympathetic, all of which leave him with deep pangs of guilt.

In what appears even more contradictory to the conventional image, Kaliyappan, who takes away life, also gives life. The rope used as a noose is burnt ritualistically by him in his prayer room and the ash from it is smeared on the forehead of the sick for a cure. In a touching scene, we see a mother with her sick infant at his doorstep on a rainy night, and the man offering his prayers and the ash. The child will be fine by daybreak, he tells her, and the relieved woman goes away. It is this Kaliyappan that society respects, and is perhaps willing to forgive for being the other Kaliyappan.

Gopalakrishnan gives his protagonist an even finer shade of humanism, when he allows him to be tormented by his conscience, which keeps reminding him that he has blood on his hands. A great devotee of the Hindu Goddess, Kali—destroyer of demons and all things evil—Kaliyappan's is in turmoil, perhaps arising out of this devotion. He is remorseful that some of those he hanged were not guilty of the crimes they had been convicted of—certainly not the last man he led to the gallows.

This mental conflict is accentuated when he is called upon by the ruler, one last time, to pull the rope. When the royal messenger arrives with the order, Kaliyappan pleads with him to spare him the cruel ordeal. 'I do not even keep well these days,' he says. But he knows that his pleas are pointless, for, as the messenger reminds him, Kaliyappan has been living on the largesse of the ruler, whose authority is boundless. Kaliyappan is crushed by the ruler's magnanimity and his own helplessness in disobeying the royal decree.

The days leading to the execution are fraught with anxiety and an acute sense of revulsion. Undertaking elaborate rituals for purification and penance, he seeks the blessings of his goddess. But peace eludes him, and we see an anguished Kaliyappan get into a bullock-cart, along with his Gandhian son, Muthu (Sunil), that will take them to the jail.

On the night before the execution, Kaliyappan is kept awake by an endless supply of liquor and stories. This is the custom: the hangman is not to sleep, because the condemned prisoner does not. The jail warder when pressed by policemen to narrate something spicy obliges them with the case of a teenaged girl raped and murdered by her brother-in-law. He escapes, but the girl's lover is held and sentenced to death.

Kaliyappan's distraught mind begins to play tricks. He imagines the girl to be his own daughter, Mallika (Reeja), and the brother-in-law, his own son-in-law, Vasu (Murali). While Vasu flees after ravishing and killing Mallika, her flute-playing lover (Sivakumar) is accused of the crime and sentenced to die. Such is Kaliyappan's state that he is even certain that the man he is to hang on the next morning is none other than Mallika's lover.

Before the night fades away, Kaliyappan is so agitated that he collapses, and his son has to take his place as the executioner. He has no choice, much like his father. However, while the elder man may not have been a Gandhian, may never have been part of India's struggle for independence, the younger man is a staunch supporter of Gandhi and is a freedom-fighter. We see him spinning the charka and wearing the white Gandhi cap. Herein lies the great dilemma, even injustice.

Adoor remarks that *Nizhalkkuthu* is about the brutality that lurks within society. One becomes a part of it whether one likes it or not. Muthu is against killing, and in a strange twist of destiny, he finds himself as a hangman. It only follows that Kaliyappan himself, given a choice, would not have been an 'envoy of death'. He is an executioner only because he has to be one.

The intense human agony and the conflict within are conveyed in *Nizhalkkuthu*. Adoor tells me that he wanted to portray the hangman as an ordinary human being, with a family, with feelings and emotions like any of us. He can feel pain, and is not one who simply executed a man and is paid for it. Sometimes, 'empathetic identification' becomes total. The hangman and the one to be hanged merge.

However, philosophical or abstract theories alone are not enough to churn out a film. There has to be something concrete, a fact or a high point in history. For, cinema, Adoor believes, must be a social document. 'It can be fiction, not fictitious.' For him, a newspaper feature on an executioner was that fact he was looking for. 'Even before I had made *Kathapurushan*, I read a story, a small feature, about the last hangman, who lived near Nagercoil. I found it very interesting. This last executioner, who was by then old, of the royal Travancore family was infrequently called to carry out the death sentence.' Of course, there were long spells in the Travancore history when hanging was abolished. This was the first state in pre-independent India to do so, though capital punishment was never permanently done away with there. Executions continue to be on free India's statute books, despite a constant plea against them.

In support of the abolitionists, I wrote an opinion-editorial piece in *The Japan Times* in January 2007—one of the many I did both for this paper and *The Hindu*. This is what it said: 'In India, although death sentence is decreed only in the rarest of rare cases, miscarriage of justice could well be significant, given the state of the judiciary, the corruption in the police force and societal complexities. The judiciary is overburdened with hundreds of legal cases pending for several years. A shortage of judges contributes to lengthy delays in the pronouncement of verdicts. An ill-paid police force seeks to better its living standards through bribery and nepotism, and a society heavily divided on the lines of religion, caste and language helps to nurture such sleaze. In a scenario such as this, cases of wilful conviction may not be exactly uncommon.

'The possibility of an innocent person being put to death is another strong factor against capital punishment. According to a 1987 Stanford University survey, at least 23 Americans were wrongly executed in the 20th century. Many escaped in the nick of time.

'In 2002, a United Nations survey concluded: "It is not prudent to accept the hypothesis that death sentence deters murder to a marginally greater extent than does the threat and application of the supposedly lesser punishment of life imprisonment."

'Absolutely so. For, can the threat of death stop a crime of passion? Can it halt a terrorist in his tracks? Can you execute a man twice?

'The erstwhile princely State of Travancore (which now forms part of Kerala) had before India's independence abolished the noose. Heavens did not fall.'

Yet, Adoor is a little undecided about the issue now. Should he be with the abolitionists or the retentionists? 'Today I am not entirely against death sentence, because I see innocent people being killed. There is no enmity between the killer and the killed. This is senseless, and I think such killers are very sick people and may be dangerous to society,' he says.

There are groups in Kerala that have gone to Gopalakrishnan to enlist his support for the abolition of the noose. 'But I have not put my signature on their memorandum, because I feel that in some cases it is foolish to allow such killers to live with others in society. This can be very dangerous. I think we need to think more about this issue,' Adoor concludes.

The idea of death by hanging occurred to him when he was shooting *Mathilukal*. There is a whole sequence on it that he created out of a single sentence in Basheer's novella, 'I stood watch over death.' He researched into it and hit upon some interesting facts. He found that often the moneyed escaped the gallows. There is an interesting observation made by an American judge who once famously said, 'Capital punishment is for those without capital.'

Gopalakrishnan's study unfolded more information. He found that the last royal Travancore executioner had a rough time. His children were born deformed and diseased. He looked very different from the image that the director carried of a hangman. 'Since my childhood I have heard stories of an executioner being ferocious to look at with bloodshot eyes. He was huge, dark, always drunk and ever in a foul mood.'

Many more fascinating pieces of information came up during the exploration. Some gruesome murders were committed even in those times, the 1940s. A particularly terrible crime was that of a man on finding his lover pregnant, killed her and dumped her body in a well.

Ultimately, *Nizhalkkuthu* turned out to be none of these. There is no evil, no brutality, and no bloodshed. (Yet one foreign critic called it 'sadistic'!) To me, it comes as a genteel story of a poor, helpless, God-fearing man driven by his ruler's command to extinguish a life. In his losing struggle against the high and the mighty, Kaliyappan is wracked by guilt, which he tries to overcome through drinking and by doing good deeds, one of which is to help cure the sick.

The movie is layered, and Kaliyappan's belief that he is a sinner translates into deep insecurity. A sign of this is his over-protectiveness towards his teenaged daughter Mallika, especially after she begins to menstruate (picturized through an elaborate ritual). He grows suspicious of even his son-in-law Vasu, who merely casts a glance at her. On the night before the final execution, Kaliyappan in his disturbed, drunken condition imagines the characters in the warder's story to be members of his own family. The man he is about to hang is Mallika's innocent lover. Such is his compassion that he finds it hard to detach himself from the execution. 'In fact, it is much more than empathy,' Adoor explains. 'He becomes a character himself in the story. So the shadow becomes real.'

Unnikrishnan's transformation into Kaliyappan is fascinating. The shadow becomes real. 'I cast him because he looks innocent, incapable of being cruel, and with a lot of sympathy for others. There is a certain hard-to-explain intensity in him. Also, I knew him well, having worked with him in *Kathapurushan*.'

Nizhalkkuthu was partly financed by the Hubert Bals Fund of the Rotterdam Film Festival, and it competed at the Venice Film Festival in 2002. *Nizhalkkuthu* was also Adoor's first work to be brought out on DVD, by San Francisco's The Global Film Initiative in 2003–04.

More recently in June 2008, London's Second Run DVD released *Elippathayam* on DVD, making it the only other movie of Gopalakrishnan's to be found on disc! A long way to go before his nine other features and several documentaries come in handy diskettes.

NIZHALKKUTHU

Cast and Credits

Year of production: 2002

Colour

Languages: Malayalam and Tamil

Duration: 90 minutes

Story, Screenplay and Direction: Adoor Gopalakrishnan

Chief Assistant: Sajeev Pillai

Producers: Adoor Gopalakrishnan Productions and Artcam International

Cinematography: Mankada Ravi Varma and Sunny Joseph

Music: Ilayaraja

Sound recording: N. Harikumar

Sound editing and mixing: Dominique Vieillard

Art Direction: Ratheesh Babu

Costumes: Satheesh S.B.

Make-up: P.N. Mani

Editing: Ajith Kumar

Cast: Oduvil Unnikrishnan (Kaliyappan), Sunil (Muthu), Reeja (Mallika) Sivakumar (Mallika's lover), Murali (Vasu)

Prizes: National Award for Best Regional Film; FIPRESCI (International Critics) Prize at Mumbai, 2003

Festivals: Venice, Rotterdam, Goteborg, Vienna, Paris, Manosque, Nantes, Fribourg, Ljubljana, Munich, London, New York, Washington DC, Toronto, Shanghai, Fukuoka and Jerusalem among others

22

Four Women

For the third time in his career of thirty-five years, Gopalakrishnan fell back on a literary work to write a script and take it to the screen. He had used Basheer's *Mathilukal* and Zacharia's *Bhaskara Pattelarum Ente Jeevithavum* (titled *Vidheyan* for the screen) with splendid success. In 2007, he tested yet another author, the late Jnanpith-award winner, Thakazhi Sivasankara Pillai. Gopalakrishnan read close to four hundred stories of his before selecting eight to make two movies, one after another, the first time ever he made two films in quick succession. In fact, there was no interval between the two at all, one shoot even overlapping the other. The crew was the same for both, though most actors were different.

Naalu Pennungal (Four Women) premiered at the Masters Section in Toronto in the fall of 2007. Of all Adoor's works, this movie has travelled to most number of festivals, nearly forty. What was particularly gratifying to the film-maker was that women audiences everywhere loved his work. Wrote the British critic Sarah Manvel in *Cinemattraction*, 'Even if they are set 60 years ago and half a world away, the stories in this movie still echo with truths about women's lives today. Short and to the point, *Four Women* is a mirror which should make us all uncomfortable with its reflection.' The film certainly transcends the barriers of time, place and culture.

As Gopalakrishnan read through Thakazhi's four hundred stories, he was touched by the stories about women. They had appeared in different collections and were written at different times. He saw great potential here—that of narrating a universal tale of the woman. Authentic and true to life as they were, the stories lent themselves to proper thematic development, convincing character delineation and formal innovation. 'It was not my intention to connect these stories through common characters or situations. I wanted to keep the stories independent of one another and at the same time build through them the progression of a theme—that of the rise of awareness in the woman,' says Adoor. 'Within each story and between the stories there is a certain passage of time (from pre-independence to post-independence India—covering a period of more than a quarter of a century).'

Naalu Pennungal has a galaxy of stars: Padmapriya, Geetu Mohandas, Nandita Das and Kavya Madhavan came together in a narrative with a strong female presence. Indeed, the four segments of this movie—'The Prostitute', 'The Virgin', 'The Housewife' and 'The Spinster'—focus on the trials and tribulations that women faced, and continue to face. Setting these stories between the mid-1940s and the mid-1960s in Kerala's verdant Kuttanad, the countryside where Thakazhi was born and grew up, Gopalakrishnan explores issues such as marital fidelity, morality and sexual desire through the plight of four women who belong to different social strata.

The four female protagonists in the four stories may appear unrelated to one another, particularly separated by time, class and social milieu, but on closer analysis we see a common thread running through each narrative: each of the protagonists is unfulfilled in a different way. The prostitute, Kunju Pennu (Padmapriya), wants to stop selling her body and even finds a man willing to live with her and take care of her, but an unfeeling and archaic system of legal justice separates the two sending them to different jails. The beat policeman, who finds them sleeping on the pavement, refuses to believe that they are man and wife, despite Kunju Pennu's desperate plea that Pappukutty (Sreejith) is her husband. Even the learned judge, who tries them, is scathingly sarcastic when he quips that two who have no home, no address and do not know who their parents are, are claiming to be man and wife. As Kunju Pennu and Pappukkuty are taken away, we realize how cruel the system can be, how unrelentingly exploitative.

'The Virgin' climbs a step higher in the social ladder: here Kumari (Geetu Mohandas) is a farm hand who is married off to an indifferent man, Narayanan (Nandulal). The marriage is not consummated, and we do not know the reason. Is he gay? Is he impotent? We have no clue, but that he is a reluctant partner is clear. In a powerful tell-all scene one night, Narayanan coldly rejects Kumari's sexual invitation. In the end, Narayanan drops Kumari at her parents' house and never returns.

Gopalakrishnan provides relief in the sombre narrative by injecting humour, though subdued and subtle. Narayanan's attention veers towards food; often the attention is singularly undivided. Narayanan's gluttonous eating tickles us no doubt, but Kumari's plight is such that the humour cannot wean us away from her.

In 'The Housewife', Chinnu Amma (Manju Pillai), may be happily married to Raman Pillai (Murali), but her home and life are rather incomplete without children. She apparently cannot have them: they die soon after their birth. When her old schoolmate, Nara Pillai (Mukesh), pays her a visit, suggests that the fault may lie with her husband and offers to help, Chinnu wavers for a moment, but quickly regains control of her senses. When she refuses him, he shoots one last question at her: what about my desire? She refuses to succumb even then.

Finally, Gopalakrishnan pushes us up to a still higher plane on the social hierarchy when he takes us into a middle-class home. Kamakshi (Nandita Das) in 'The Spinster' finds herself being passed over by a prospective groom (Ravi Vallathol), who chooses her more attractive younger sister, Subhadra (Kavya Madhavan). Years later, when her mother dies, the unmarried Kamakshi finds herself alone and is forced to live with Subhadra. But soon Kamakshi is compelled to leave Subhadra after her jealous outbursts, and returns to her ancestral house to live by herself.

This story is bracketed between two door knocks—one seen from outside the door and the other heard inside the room. After several agonizing moments when Kamakshi stands facing the door, hearing the knocks and debating whether to let in the man she had invited earlier, she asks him to go away. Does she find peace when she stops herself from yielding to sexual temptation? Possibly. But, I suppose, what is more pertinent is that she resolves to face the world without a man.

These stories amply illuminate society's indifference towards women. The community is inconsiderate, even hostile, when women make unconventional choices. The judge cannot understand how a streetwalker can live with a poor man and make a home.

When Narayanan sends Kumari back to her parents' home, she is blamed for the break-up. Scandals spread. But the man is absolved. Her parents are foxed when she tells them that there had been no marriage at all in the first place.

Raman Pillai (Murali), Chinnu's gentle and caring husband, is unwilling to accept that he could be responsible for the premature death of her babies. Nara Pillai is hurt and annoyed when a woman craving for children could turn down a stud like him.

It is neither Kamakshi's fault nor choice that she has to lead the life of a spinster. It is the unfair social system which treats woman as an adjunct of man that is responsible for her humiliating predicament. As an unmarried woman, Kamakshi finds her status in her own house taking a beating.

Despite their adversities, these women are no weepy creatures. They have a certain inherent strength that probably comes from Kerala's matrilineal society, where women enjoyed greater privileges and a higher status than those elsewhere in the country.

Before selecting Thakazhi's stories, Gopalakrishnan had toyed with the idea of making into a film the author's novel, *Kayaru* (Coir), which traces Travancore's history during the past 200 years, and there are hundreds of characters in it. 'Initially, I thought I would take a segment out of it and make it into a movie. But then I did not find it suitable with its innumerable characters and incidents,' Adoor explains why he eventually settled for Thakazhi's short stories.

Of the eight he chose, the first four stories run thematically. They are about women, and this is the most obvious thread connecting one to another. When he arranged them in a definite social hierarchical order—from the lowliest prostitute to an agricultural labourer to a lower-middle-class housewife to a single woman from the middling rungs of the middle-class—the link became stronger and pronounced. Thakazhi could never have imagined that some day someone would pick his stories and create a theme out of them.

An undercurrent of sex is another feature that binds these stories. It is evident in the first story of 'The Prostitute'. In the others, we see a negation, denial of it and so on. However, sex remains well below the surface, and there is no attempt to sensationalize it.

Shot in the backwaters of Alappuzha, the boat appears time and again in *Naalu Pennungal*. The placid calm of the waters is occasionally disturbed by a slow-moving boat. For Gopalakrishnan, the boat and the river are part of his indelible memory that he carries from his childhood, when he stood watching day after day a priest pass by in a tiny boat.

The richness of the region—the greenery and the sheer scenic beauty—has been captured vividly by the cinematographer Radhakrishnan, the subject of women, with their colour and vivaciousness (despite their suffering) adding value to the imagery. *Naalu Pennungal* is the most colourful in Gopalakrishnan's body of work.

Radhakrishnan had worked on two of Gopalakrishnan's documentaries, but *Naalu Pennungal* was the first feature. Of Gopalakrishnan's eleven features, Mankada Ravi Varma had been his cinematographer for the first nine. Even when the ninth feature, *Nizhalkkuthu*, was being made, Mankada had been unwell, and the cameraman Sunny Joseph was asked to stand by.

Gopalakrishnan shared a unique bond with Mankada, who enjoyed the rare privilege of being the only one among the entire cast and crew to read the script before principal photography began. I could notice the depth of this relationship and the understanding between them when I accompanied Gopalakrishnan one evening to see an ailing Mankada in his Chennai home. He came out of his bedroom and sat with us for a while. The two hardly spoke. They did not have to. But when we were leaving Mankada's home, I could clearly see sadness in his eyes, as I could see in Gopalakrishnan's too. To me, at that moment, it seemed like the end of an era, when the Adoor–Mankada partnership produced some great cinema.

NAALU PENNUNGAL

Cast and Credits

Year of production: 2007

Colour

Language: Malayalam

Duration: 105 minutes

Screenplay and Direction: Adoor Gopalakrishnan

Story: Thakazhi Sivasankara Pillai

Chief Assistant: Meera Sahib

Producer: Adoor Gopalakrishnan

Co-producer: Benzy Martin; production partly supported by Doordarshan

Cinematography: M.J. Radhakrishnan

Music: Isaac Thomas

Sound: N. Harikumar

Art Direction: Rajasekharan

Costumes: S.B. Satheesh

Make-up: P.N. Mani

Editing: Ajith Kumar

Cast: Padmapriya (Kunju. Pennu), Sreejith (Pappukkutty), Geetu Mohandas (Kumari), Nandulal (Narayanan), Manju Pillai (Chinnu Amma), Murali (Raman Pillai), Mukesh (Nara Pillai), Nandita Das (Kamakshi), Kavya Madhavan (Subhadra), Ravi Vallathol (Subhadra's husband)

Prizes: National Award for the Best Director

Festivals: Toronto, New York, New Jersey, Washington DC, Los Angeles, Seattle, Miami, Palm Springs, Vancouver, Trinidad, London, Warsaw, Madrid, Barcelona, Nantes, Deauville, Manosque, Rotterdam, Munich, Hamburg, Goteborg, Ljubljana, Brussels, Vienna, Jerusalem, Dubai, Cairo, Brisbane, Hong Kong and Dhaka among others

23

A Climate for Crime

Gopalakrishnan must have got fond of Thakazhi. Even before *Naalu Pennungal* went on the floors, he had selected another set of four short stories of the Jnanpith award–winning writer, scripted them, titled them *Oru Pennum Randaanum* (A Climate for Crime) and began filming it soon after he wrapped up *Naalu Pennungal*. 'What interested me is that they are basically excellent human stories,' Adoor explains. 'One of the four, "The Police", is a complete story. Fleshed out, I think this is one of the entirely worked out short story I adapted from amongst his body of literature. "The Police" has been penned in such detail that I did not have to add or delete much unlike in the seven other (four in *Naalu Pennungal*) stories, where I worked on plot development, characterization, situations and interpretations.'

Set in the 1940s Kerala, 'The Police' underlines corruption in the force, an evil that persists in post-independence India. When a strict police inspector (played by Vijayaraghavan) is posted at a station, head constable Kuttan Pillai (Jagannathan) and constable Mathu (Nedumudi Venu) are on the boil, having led a long life of sleaze. They had run the police station as their fiefdom. Pressured by the inspector to solve a criminal case that the two had wrapped up after taking a hefty bribe from the suspect, they strike it lucky as they drink in a local bar. A rickshaw-puller (Krishnakumar), also at the bar, finds himself in prison as the accused in the case, his savings he had with him to buy a rickshaw taken away by the two cops. Forced to confess to a crime he did not commit, the rickshaw-puller is sentenced to six months of hard labour in prison.

This tale conveys the pathos through the comic. Convinced by Mathu that his jail term would be a mere ten days, the puller is shattered and helpless when he hears the judge sentencing him to a much longer period. Why did he not at the point cry out that injustice was being meted out to him? Probably, his illiteracy and the power of the uniform, which can be quite intimidating.

However, the narrative sits lightly on us, the underlying humour providing a real laugh. I particularly liked the way both Jagannathan and Venu perform their parts: the scene when they are hauled up by the inspector has such understated wit that I hardly felt I was watching a serious plot, and it was one. Police corruption and brutality (there is nothing physical here except for a brief minute or two at the bar) are serious issues, and Gopalakrishnan deals with them effectively without adding any melodramatic element to them. There is no emotional outburst, no weeping, and the rickshaw-puller stoically walks into the policemen's net and later into prison.

'The Police' is the second of the four segments: the first is called 'The Thief', the third 'Two Men and a Woman' and the fourth, 'One Woman, Two Men'.

Adoor says, 'The four segments tell stories independent of one another. What connects them is the recurring theme of crime. Starting from simple, parable-like tales about ordinary people, the narrative slowly takes on questions of longing, love and life, culminating in the story of the contemporary legend of Panki, the irresistible village beauty. Unlike my earlier works, I have used dialogue predominantly to comment, endorse or simply report on the development of the plot, a dramatic epic device effectively used in the Mahabharata.'

An extremely poignant story is that of 'The Thief'. Adoor was deeply touched by this, and 'it is only then can you feel a strong sense of empathy with the characters'. Little Kunjunni (Amal Jose) is angst-ridden to see his father, Neelantan (M.R. Gopakumar), being frequently incarcerated for theft. Yet, he cannot help stealing, because he cannot find a job. In a scene where we see his desperation, he tells his neighbour, Mathai (Indran) that he really has no choice. If he does not steal, his family would starve. But Kunjunni is as much grieved when his classmate at school ridicules him about Neelantan. Finally, a petition by Mathai and some influential people of the area ensures that Neelantan is locked up for a long time.

The story narrated through the boy's eyes—and heart—has a powerful moral undertone of crime and punishment. And as Kunjunni feels and Mathai verbalizes, theft is sin. Gopalakrishnan steers clear of taking a stand here, for that might have led to a question that Neelantan himself poses: 'I do not want to steal. But then I cannot get a job, and how then do I feed myself and my family?'

Like the other three, 'The Thief' is set in the 1940s Travancore. World War II was devastating most of Europe, and it cast an ominous shadow on British India. Shortage of food, clothing, petrol and kerosene was making life for especially the poor Indian hard. Grains were hoarded and sold to those who could pay high prices. Rampant unemployment was fuelling the fire of crime and avarice, and the four stories relate to misdemeanours committed not only by the deprived but also the comparatively privileged landed gentry.

'The Thief' ends with a sheer dramatic moment, when Kunjunni returns home from school one afternoon to find a pair of new clothes and a delicious spread of food awaiting him. He knows that his father must have broken out of jail and stolen again (possibly from Mathai's house as there had been a burglary there) to give him the goodies. He had earlier got his mother (Seema G. Nair) to promise that together they would stop Neelantan from leading this shameful life. Kunjunni is distraught.

However Neelantan is not all dark. None of Gopalakrishnan's characters is. Neelantan is a man pushed to the wall. And he does exude some fairness in his foul deeds: he warns Mathai that he ought to be careful with his possessions. Mathai is. But Neelantan knows his craft well, and is proud of it. He breaks into Mathai's house—that is what one is given to understand—after escaping from prison, where he has been kept possibly unlawfully after the petition by citizens asking the police to keep him under detention to stop him from committing any more thefts.

In the third segment, 'Two Men and a Woman', a young university student, Krishnankutty, played by Sudheesh, has casual romance with a sweeper-girl, which leads to sex and pregnancy. He is desperate, because he knows that a scandal of this sort will cause immense trouble in his family. His uncle, who supports him by paying him his tuition fee, would stop his allowances and his education. When the girl agrees to abort her foetus, he goes to his advocate friend (Jagadeesh), and together they make a journey by river to a quack (P.C. Soman) whose concoction of a potion can terminate a pregnancy. The two men return after asking the quack to prepare the medicine.

However, a little later, it turns out that the girl was never pregnant, and that it was a false alarm. This dilemma helps Krishnankutty to see things clearly, and he makes a difficult choice. But he is happy.

In a way, this story (as do the others) rings true, for Thakazhi wove his fiction from what he heard, saw or experienced in his lifetime. He worked for sometime as a law court pleader in Ambalapuzha, near Alappuzha, in Kerala.

Originally titled, 'A Friend', it was not even a short story, but part of Thakazhi's collection of profiles, where he talks about a few phases from his past. 'Two Men and a Woman' is an extremely minimalist work: the girl is never seen or heard. Not to be missed is the message: a boy from the higher echelons of society understands the implication of deserting a girl, and he ultimately crosses the caste and economic barrier.

Although Adoor contends that he was careful enough to choose only those stories of Thakazhi that were not so well known he could not help selecting 'One Woman, Two Men', which is fairly popular. In Kerala's matrilineal society, women enjoyed some rights uncommon elsewhere. Panki (Praveena) is a woman of grace and beauty, and men are smitten by her. Among them is Rama Kurup (Ravi Vallathol) who forsakes everything to marry her. But the relationship is obviously problematic: she is young and he is old, and like perhaps many old men with young wives, Kurup is so possessive that he even asks Panki not to laugh loudly. When men stop outside his house for a harmless chat, he shoos them away. He does not even care when they ridicule him.

Kurup's fears come true when he finds Panki's lover, Kittu Kurup (Manoj K. Jayan), one night in their room, and in anger he stabs him. The lover survives, and Kurup is arrested, but released on bail. However, things take a very different turn when the families of the two men clash, causing deaths. The court takes a serious view of this and imprisons both Kurup and the lover for three years. They serve the term together, and when they return to Panki, a shock awaits them.

There is a marvellous twist at the end, and Gopalakrishnan's script keeps a few incidents off the screen. For, instance, we do not see Kurup finding Panki with her lover. We do not see one stabbing the other, nor are we shown the clash between the families. All these are told by an elderly woman to her bedridden husband, and these narrations explain the drama played out between Panki and her two men.

Praveena was slightly uncomfortable playing the part of a woman with multiple love interests. She kept asking Adoor whether she was a 'bad woman'. Adoor reassured her saying that she was only being 'natural'.

Gopalakrishnan added his inputs to most of the stories here. They are no straight word-to-picture transfers. 'I am not trying to negate or underestimate Thakazhi's worth. I like what he wrote. I respect that. But I think this is also my work. It does become mine when it is crafted into a movie,' Adoor says. 'It is a free adaptation, not a literal one.'

Although there are no common characters in the last two films—*Naalu Pennungal* and *Oru Pennum Randaanum*—there are a few institutions which are common to both: the police station, the court, and the liquor shop and of course the Kuttanad landscapes with vast paddy fields and long stretches of water around it. 'Making these two movies based on short stories was quite a challenge because a good short story is invariably about one idea that is etched economically in words. When you attempt to make a film based on it, suddenly it turns out to offer several possibilities at the same time. So, one needs to take the liberty of redrawing its contours all anew keeping the basic idea for inspiration, but proceeding on your own without fear or doubts of transgressing the terrain of the writer,' Adoor surmises.

ORU PENNUM RANDAANUM

Cast and Credits

Year of Production: 2008

Colour

Language: Malayalam

Duration: 115 minutes

Screenplay and Direction: Adoor Gopalakrishnan

Story: Thakazhi Sivasankara Pillai

Chief Assistant: Meera Sahib

Producer: Adoor Gopalakrishnan

Co-producer: Benzy Martin; production partly supported by Doordarshan

Cinematography: M.J. Radhakrishnan

Music: Isaac Thomas

Sound: Krishnanunni and N. Harikumar

Art Direction: Rajasekharan

Costumes: S.B. Satheesh

Make-up: P.N. Mani

Editing: Ajith Kumar

Cast: M.R. Gopakumar (Neelantan), Seema G. Nair (Neelantan's wife), Master Amal, Jose (Kunjunni), Indran (Mathai) Nedumudi Venu (Mathu), Jagannathan (Kuttan Pillai), Vijayaraghavan (police inspector), Krishnakumar (rickshaw-puller), Praveena (Panki), Ravi Vallathol (Rama Kurup), Manoj K. Jayan (Kittu Kurup), Sudheesh (Krishnankutty), Jagadeesh (advocate), P.C. Soman (quack)

Prizes: Kerala State Awards for Best Film, Best Director, Best Script, Best Sound (Krishnanunni and N. Harikumar) and Best Supporting Actress (Praveena)

Festivals: New Jersey, Houston, Washington DC, Rotterdam, Freiberg, Madrid, Rome, Split, Dubai, Tampa and Mumbai and Goa among others

Index

211